Anti-Terrorism Law and Foreign Terrorist Fighters

The emergence of Islamic State has created new security concerns for Western nations, particularly those which have experienced a recent upsurge in domestic terrorist activities inspired by the organisation. Whilst the nature of the terrorist threat might have changed since the early days after 9/11, domestic responses to that threat—in the form of new anti-terrorism laws— have not demonstrated a significant evolution in thinking about counter-terrorism. Many of the measures introduced in Australia and the UK since the emergence of the foreign terrorist fighters crisis have simply updated pre-existing regimes, such as control orders in Australia and Terrorism Prevention and Investigation Measures in the UK. Others have been more innovative, such as the Australian offence of entering a declared terrorist zone. What all the responses have in common, however, is that they think inside the proverbial box; that is, the Australian and UK Parliaments continue to be of the view that enacting new and increasingly intrusive legislation is the best way of resolving the threat of terrorism.

Anti-Terrorism Law and Foreign Terrorist Fighters evaluates whether the new legislation introduced in Australia and the UK is, in fact, necessary, appropriate, or effective at dealing with the foreign terrorist fighters phenomenon. It will be of value to academics and students who teach, research, and study the ever-evolving area of anti-terrorism law and counter-terrorism policy, and of interest to scholars in a number of fields including law, comparative politics and government, and terrorism and security studies.

Jessie Blackbourn is a Research Fellow at the Centre for Socio-Legal Studies at the University of Oxford, UK.

Deniz Kayis is currently the Associate for Chief Justice Allsop AO of the Federal Court of Australia.

Nicola McGarrity is a Senior Lecturer and the Director of the Terrorism Law Reform Project at the University of New South Wales, Australia.

Routledge Research in Terrorism and the Law

Anti-Terrorism Law and Foreign Terrorist Fighters

Jessie Blackbourn,
Deniz Kayis and
Nicola McGarrity

Routledge
Taylor & Francis Group

LONDON AND NEW YORK

First published 2018 by Routledge

2 Park Square, Milton Park, Abingdon, Oxfordshire OX14 4RN

52 Vanderbilt Avenue, New York, NY 10017

Routledge is an imprint of the Taylor & Francis Group, an informa business

First issued in paperback 2019

Library of Congress Cataloging-in-Publication Data
Names: Blackbourn, Jessie, editor. | Kayis, Deniz, editor. |
    McGarrity, Nicola, editor.
Title: Anti-terrorism law and foreign terrorist fighters / Edited by Jessie
    Blackbourn, Deniz Kayis and Nicola McGarrity.
Description: New York, NY : Routledge, 2018. | Series: Routledge research in
    terrorism and the law | Includes index.
Identifiers: LCCN 2017053087| ISBN 9781138093379 (hardback) |
    ISBN 9781315106878 (web pdf) | ISBN 9781351605434 (epub) |
    ISBN 9781351605427 (mobipocket)
Subjects: LCSH: Terrorism—Prevention—Law and legislation |
    Terrorism—Prevention—Law and legislation—Australia. |
    Terrorism—Prevention—Law and legislation—Great Britain. |
    Terrorists—Legal status, laws, etc.
Classification: LCC KZ7220 .A9578 2018 | DDC 344.4105/325—dc23
LC record available at https://lccn.loc.gov/2017053087

ISBN: 978-1-138-09337-9 (hbk)
ISBN: 978-0-367-89041-4 (pbk)

Typeset in Times New Roman
by Apex CoVantage, LLC

Contents

Acknowledgments

The authors owe a continuing debt of gratitude to Professor George Williams AO for his generous mentoring.

Drs Jessie Blackbourn and Nicola McGarrity benefitted immensely from their membership of the ARC Laureate Fellowship: Anti-Terror Laws and the Democratic Challenge, led by Professor Williams, and in particular being challenged by him to respond to the big questions regarding anti-terrorism lawmaking in Australia, the UK, and other jurisdictions. It is in discussions with Professor Williams and the other members of the Laureate Project that the seeds for the analytical approach taken in this book were sewn.

Furthermore, in her capacity as a Scientia Scholar at the University of New South Wales, Ms Deniz Kayis was mentored by Professor Williams. He also supervised and examined her honours thesis, upon which the discussion of citizenship powers in Chapter 4 of this book was based.

We also want to acknowledge the input of Dr Tamara Tulich. Her discussions with Dr Blackbourn have been invaluable in framing the analysis of Australia's system of control orders in Chapter 3.

Last, but certainly not least, we thank Ms Sharon Mo for her hard work and dedication to the editing of this book.

Author Biographies

Jessie Blackbourn is a Research Fellow in the Centre for Socio-Legal Studies at the University of Oxford, and Honorary Fellow at the Law School, University of Western Australia. Her first monograph, *Anti-Terrorism Law and Normalising Northern Ireland,* was published by Routledge-Cavendish in 2014.

Deniz Kayis is currently the Associate for Chief Justice Allsop AO of the Federal Court of Australia. She completed her combined Bachelor's degree in Arts and Law at the University of New South Wales in 2017, where she was a recipient of the prestigious Scientia Scholarship and graduated with Honours Class 1.

Nicola McGarrity is a Senior Lecturer in Public and Criminal Law at the University of New South Wales. She is also the Director of the Terrorism Law Reform Project in the Gilbert + Tobin Centre of Public Law. Nicola has published extensively on comparative anti-terrorism law and policy, as well as working as a barrister in this field.

Glossary

AFP	Australian Federal Police
ASIO	Australian Security Intelligence Organisation
AUSTRAC	Australian Transaction Reports and Analysis Centre
BBC	British Broadcasting Corporation
Citizenship Act	Citizenship Act 2007 (Cth)
COAG	Council of Australian Governments
Counter-Terrorism Amendment Act	Counter-Terrorism Legislation Amendment Act (No 1) 2016 (Cth)
Counter-Terrorism Amendment Bill	Counter-Terrorism Legislation Amendment Bill (No 1) 2016 (Cth)
Court of Appeal	Court of Appeal for England and Wales
Criminal Code	Criminal Code Act 1995 (Cth)
CTS Act	Counter-Terrorism and Security Act 2015 (UK)
CTS Bill	Counter-Terrorism and Security Bill 2014 HC Bill (2014–15) (UK)
Department of Immigration	Australian Department of Immigration and Border Protection
ECHR	European Convention on Human Rights
EU	European Union
Foreign Evidence Act	Foreign Evidence Act 1994 (Cth)
Foreign Fighters Act	Counter-Terrorism Legislation (Foreign Fighters) Act 2014 (Cth)
Foreign Fighters Bill	Counter-Terrorism Legislation (Foreign Fighters) Bill 2014 (Cth)
Foreign Incursions Act	Crimes (Foreign Incursions and Recruitment) Act 1978 (Cth)

FTRO	Foreign Travel Restriction Order
Home Secretary	Secretary of State for the Home Department (UK)
HRA	Human Rights Act 1998 (UK)
ICCPR	International Covenant on Civil and Political Rights
INSLM	Independent National Security Legislation Monitor
IRA	Irish Republican Army
IRTL	Independent Reviewer of Terrorism Legislation
Minister for Immigration	Australian Minister for Immigration and Border Protection
NSIA	National Security Information (Criminal and Civil Proceedings) Act 2004 (Cth)
PJCHR	Parliamentary Joint Committee on Human Rights (Australia)
PJCIS	Parliamentary Joint Committee on Intelligence and Security (Australia)
PTA	Prevention of Terrorism Act 2005 (UK)
RUSI	Royal United Services Institute
SIAC	Special Immigration Appeals Commission
TA 2000	Terrorism Act 2000 (UK)
TA 2006	Terrorism Act 2006 (UK)
TEO	Temporary Exclusion Order
TPIMs	Terrorism Prevention and Investigation Measures
TPIMs Act	Terrorism Prevention and Investigation Measures Act 2011 (UK)
UK	United Kingdom
UN	United Nations
UN Charter Act	Charter of the United Nations Act 1945 (Cth)
UNSC	United Nations Security Council
US	United States
YPG	Kurdish People's Defence Forces
YPJ	Kurdish Women's Protection Units

1   Introduction

Just after 10.30pm on 22 May 2017, as more than 14,000 people were leaving a performance by American pop singer Ariana Grande, an improvised explosive device was detonated in the foyer of the Manchester Arena. The detonation killed 23 people and injured another 250. One of those killed was the suicide bomber, Salman Ramadan Abedi. There was then—and indeed continues to be—some confusion about the extent to which the UK authorities were aware of Abedi's activities prior to the bombing.[1] He had been arrested in 2012 for minor criminal offences. The British Broadcasting Corporation (BBC) also reported that acquaintances of Abedi at Manchester College had called an anti-terrorism hotline expressing concern about his extremist views. Any knowledge of these calls was denied by the Greater Manchester Police; however, the UK's domestic intelligence agency, MI5, has since commenced a review of its processes in light of confirmation by the callers.[2] An independent report of MI5 and police internal reviews was also released in December 2017. This report, by former Independent Reviewer of Terrorism Legislation (IRTL) David Anderson, clarified that while Abedi was a peripheral subject of interest, he was not under investigation at the time of the attack. He was classed as a 'closed' subject of interest of 'low residual risk', meaning he was no longer assessed as representing a national security threat. However, Abedi had also recently been identified as one of a 'small number of individuals ... who merited further examination'. This further examination as to the threat posed by Abedi was due to take place on 31 May 2017, a mere nine days after the Manchester Arena terrorist attack.[3]

The unfortunate reality is that terrorism is nothing new (nor indeed even unexpected) in the UK. That country has been grappling with the threat posed by terrorism for over a century. The critical point, however, insofar as the modern threat of terrorism is concerned, is the increasing percentage of terrorist attacks with links to international terrorist organisations, especially Islamic State,[4] Al-Qaida, and their affiliates. This may be contrasted with the concentration upon Northern Irish terrorism from the early 1970s to the late 1990s. Two months prior to the bombing of the Manchester Arena, Khalid Masood drove a car along the pavement at Westminster Bridge, killing five pedestrians before abandoning the car and fatally stabbing a police constable. A further three terrorist attacks have occurred in the UK in 2017, all but one of which—the attack near the Muslim Welfare House in Finsbury Park in June 2017—bear some connection to Islamic State.

Australia is in a similar position. Since December 2014, there have been at least five terrorist attacks on Australian soil. With just one exception, being the arson committed at the Imam Ali Islamic Centre in December 2016, each of these may be attributed to Islamic State. These attacks are; the stabbing of two police officers outside the Endeavour Hills police station in September 2014; the Lindt café siege in December 2014; the murder of police accountant, Curtis Cheng, in October 2015; and the stabbing of a member of the public in Minto in regional New South Wales in September 2016. A sixth incident, namely, the shooting of one person and holding of another hostage at an apartment complex in Melbourne in June 2017, has also been described by the current Independent National Security Legislation Monitor (INSLM), James Renwick, as an act of terrorism.[5] However, George Williams has written that '[w]e cannot be certain, and may never know, whether he was involved in an act of terrorism or if his actions were merely those of a violent, drug-affected man'.[6]

In many instances, attribution to Islamic State has been straightforward in that responsibility has been explicitly claimed by the organisation. Indeed, in respect of the bombing at the Manchester Arena, Islamic State published not one, but two claims of responsibility. The first described the attacker as a 'soldier of the Khilafah [caliphate]', and the other identified a 'security detachment' as responsible.[7] However, even in these supposedly 'easy' cases, the authorities in the relevant jurisdiction have gone on to undertake the complex task of mapping the relationship between the attacker and Islamic State. Where the attacker has been charged and brought before the courts, undertaking this task has been necessary to prove the motivational element of the definition of terrorism to the criminal standard of beyond a reasonable doubt.[8] Such trials have, however, been the exception rather than the rule. This is because the majority of those who have committed terrorist attacks in Australia and the UK have been killed in the course of those incidents. Nevertheless, investigations into the relationship between the perpetrator and Islamic State have still been undertaken by the authorities for the dual purposes of identifying any accomplices, as well as better understanding the processes of radicalisation and thus what can be done to minimise the risk of homegrown terrorism.

It is these investigations which have occupied the time of UK intelligence and law enforcement agencies in the aftermath of the terrorist attack at the Manchester Arena. In the course of their investigations, evidence emerged that Abedi, a Mancunian of Libyan descent, had met with operatives of the Katibat al-Battar al-Libi during a trip to Libya shortly before the attack.[9] This group, which was formed by Libyans who had fought in the previous Iraq and Afghanistan conflicts, provided one of the first contingents of foreigners to arrive in Syria in 2012. Since pledging allegiance to Islamic State leader, Abu Bakr Al-Baghdadi, Katibat al-Battar al-Libi has also been linked to attacks throughout Europe. These include the synchronised attacks in Paris on 13 November 2015 which killed 130 people, and the attack by Anis Amra upon a Christmas market in Berlin in December 2016.[10] Although the evidence is not conclusive—and, given his death, likely never will be—Abedi is suspected of having been trained in the use of explosives by the Libyan group with the intention of returning to the UK to commit a terrorist act. In other words, he was a returned 'foreign terrorist fighter'.

Despite the co-opting of this phrase by politicians and the media to describe Westerners involved in the current Syrian and Iraqi conflicts, the phenomenon of people participating in foreign conflicts has a long history. It goes back at least as far as the early Viking invasions, the twelfth- and thirteenth-century Crusades, the involvement of Guy Fawkes in the 1605 Gunpowder Plot, the American Revolution, the Spanish Civil War, and the involvement of the Mujahedeen in the Soviet-Afghan War.[11] Many—if not most—of these historical examples would fall within the definition of 'foreign terrorist fighters' provided by the United Nations Security Council (UNSC) in Resolution 2178.[12] The catalyst for the adoption of this Resolution on 24 September 2014 was the 'particular concern that foreign terrorist fighters are being recruited by and are joining entities such as the Islamic State, . . . the Al-Nusrah Front . . . and other cells, affiliates, splinter groups or derivatives of Al-Qaida'.[13] However, the definition goes far beyond this to include any

> individuals who travel to a State other than their States of residence or nationality for the purpose of the perpetration, planning, or preparation of, or participation in, terrorist acts or the providing or receiving of terrorist training, including in connection with armed conflict.[14]

Not only does the breadth of this definition make it clear that the challenges posed by foreign terrorist fighters in the modern era have historical precedents, but it also forces a reconsideration of the prevailing stereotypes about the role of such fighters in the Syrian and Iraqi conflicts. In understanding the challenges that Australia and the UK face, as well as the effectiveness of their legislative responses to those challenges, the heterogeneity of the foreign terrorist fighters phenomenon as manifested in these conflicts must be borne in mind. The definition in Resolution 2178 does not refer to any specific terrorist organisation (albeit that concern about Islamic State, the Al-Nusrah Front, Al-Qaida, and their affiliates was part of the context in which it was adopted). Not all the individuals who have travelled to Syria and Iraq did so for the purpose of supporting the aforementioned organisations.

In contrast to the stereotype of the foreign terrorist fighter, many individuals participated in the Syrian conflict in its early stages, prior to the advent of

Islamic State. The Syrian civil war commenced in March 2011, in response to President Bashar-al-Assad's suppression of peaceful protests occurring as part of the Arab Spring. However, Islamic State was not formed for another two years. That organisation quickly achieved military success, taking over the Syrian city of Raqqa in March 2013, followed by the second largest city in Iraq, Mosul, in June the following year. Several months later, Islamic State declared a caliphate in Iraq and Syria and claimed authority over the world's Muslims. In addition to the early participants, other individuals have travelled to the conflict zones since April 2013—when the organisation was formed—to fight against it. The difficulty, so far as the legitimacy of such activities is concerned, is that most of the opponents of Islamic State, such as the Kurdish YPG (People's Defence Forces) and YPJ (Women's Protection Units), are themselves characterised as terrorist organisations.

Another facet of the heterogeneity of the phenomenon is that not all foreign terrorist fighters are—in spite of what that phrase might suggest—actually engaged in combat. There is a spectrum of involvement which ranges from those fighting on the front line, to children who were taken by their parents to the conflict zones, or were even born there. For example, in January 2016, an unnamed woman from Bradford in the UK was sentenced to more than five years imprisonment for attempting to travel to Syria with her two children without their father's consent. In sentencing the woman, Justice Jameson stated:

> The fate of your children would have been either to have subscribed, fully and actively, as we have all seen in the appalling use of a young child in an IS propaganda video in recent days, to such behaviour, or to have suffered it themselves. . . . This was a terrible betrayal of your responsibilities to your children and of their trust in you.[15]

Sitting somewhere in the grey area between individuals engaged in combat and innocent children are those who provide forms of support to Islamic State, Al-Qaida, and their affiliates behind the front line, such as medical assistance and operation of its extensive propaganda machinery. A particularly significant problem in the UK has been the travel of more than 50 young women to Syria and Iraq to marry foreign terrorist fighters and become the mothers of a next generation of fighters.[16]

This book does not challenge the core of the position taken by the authorities in both Australia and the UK that the foreign terrorist fighters phenomenon as manifested in the Syrian and Iraqi conflicts 'demands specific and targeted measures to mitigate this threat'.[17] This phenomenon should not be dismissed as simply one aspect of the general threat posed by terrorism in the twenty-first century. Nor should it be regarded as indistinguishable from historical precedents like those already mentioned above. As the Home Secretary, Amber Rudd, informed the UK Parliament on 22 June 2017: 'We now believe we are experiencing a new trend in the threat we face'.[18] The number of Westerners, including from Australia and the UK, who have travelled to Syria and Iraq in recent years represents a significant increase upon the numbers involved in other conflicts in the modern era. In June 2014, the Soufan Group estimated that more than 12,000 foreign terrorist fighters from 81 countries had travelled to Syria to join the conflict. Of those, 3,000 were from Western countries.[19] By December 2015, the conflict had spread to Iraq, and the number of foreign terrorist fighters had more than doubled, to somewhere between 27,000 and 31,000 foreign terrorist fighters, including more than 10,000 Westerners.[20] Less than one year later, on 2 June 2016, a US State Department official reported that intelligence estimates put over 40,000 foreign terrorist fighters from over 100 countries as having travelled to the Syrian and Iraqi conflicts.[21]

Accepting that a direct and targeted response is necessary, this book evaluates the effectiveness of the legislative responses to this phenomenon in Australia and the UK. The concentration upon legislation—as opposed to non-legislative, civil society, and military responses—is apt given that this has been the default official reaction to the threat of terrorism in both jurisdictions. In the UK, anti-terrorism legislation was first enacted in 1974 in response to a campaign of Irish Republican Army (IRA) bombings in mainland Britain.[22] That legislation was amended and extended in response to further terrorist attacks in the 1980s and 1990s, and new legislation was introduced following the Omagh bombing by the Real IRA in August 1998.[23] This pattern of reactive lawmaking was continued with the enactment of legislation after the September 11 terrorist attacks in New York and Washington,[24] the July 2005 London bombings[25] and, most recently, in response to the threat posed by foreign terrorist fighters.[26] Australia's response to terrorism has followed a similar path, although its legislation has—until very recently—generally been a response to terrorist attacks overseas rather than on domestic soil. Indeed, in his 2011 book, *The 9/11 Effect*, Kent Roach went so far as to describe the pattern of lawmaking in Australia as one of 'hyperlegislation'.[27]

In seeking to deal with the foreign terrorist fighters phenomenon, Australia and the UK have relied upon a combination of pre-existing legislative measures as well as those specifically enacted in response to the phenomenon. This book directs its attention to both categories of legislation. It does so by focusing on three types of measures enacted or amended in response to the foreign terrorist fighters phenomenon: criminal measures (Chapter 2); hybrid sanctions (Chapter 3); and immigration and citizenship laws (Chapter 4). This book does not simply provide an overview of these legislative measures, but it also draws lessons about their effectiveness in the long term in light of the manner in which they have been utilised to date. In so doing, it emphasises the complexity of the foreign terrorist fighters phenomenon and the need to avoid simplistic responses that take a one-size-fits-all approach. This book does not limit itself to the prevailing stereotype of the foreign terrorist fighter as a Westerner who travels to the Syrian or Iraqi conflicts to fight alongside Islamic State. Instead, it calls attention to the diverse challenges which the phenomenon poses, especially in so far as young people (whether sympathisers on domestic soil or those who are caught up in the conflict zones) and opponents of Islamic State are concerned. It is by extending the field of vision to these areas that systemic problems with the default reliance upon legislation in Australia and the UK are revealed.

There has been little reflexivity from the Australian and UK Governments as to whether this default reliance on new legislation is actually an appropriate response to terrorism in general, and to the foreign terrorist fighters phenomenon in particular. As Fiona de Londras commented:

> The (generally put) trend in counter-terrorism tends to be to implement measures, and then to implement more measures, and then more, with little or no assessment of the effectiveness and impacts of these policies, laws, instruments and approaches or, sometimes, of their necessity.[28]

Albeit that concrete evidence in support has often been missing, the language of effectiveness has been front and centre in political claims about the necessity for introducing or amending legislation in response to the foreign terrorist fighters phenomenon. This book, by utilising that same concept of 'effectiveness' as a yardstick, seeks to engage with ongoing policy debates about the best way to respond to this phenomenon.

In the most basic sense, something is effective if it produces the desired outcome. Legislation is no different. It is effective if it produces the intended result. The intended result of anti-terrorism legislation can be identified by examining parliament's stated purpose for enacting it. Typically, in the Australian and UK contexts, the justification for legislative responses to the threat of terrorism has been to prevent the commission of terrorist attacks or to facilitate the prosecution of those who are suspected of involvement in terrorism-related activity. Parliamentarians have emphasised the need for 'strengthening', 'facilitating' and 'enhancing' the laws to ensure that they 'work' to prevent terrorism and keep the country safe. For example, in a statement to the Australian Federal Parliament on 22 September 2014, the then Prime Minister, Tony Abbott, stated:

> My unambiguous message to all Australians who fight with terrorist groups is that you will be arrested, prosecuted and jailed for a very

long time; and that our laws are being changed to make it easier to keep potential terrorists off our streets.[29]

In introducing draft legislation several days later, the Attorney-General, George Brandis, described it as 'an important step in the Government's continuing efforts to strengthen Australia's robust national security laws to proactively and effectively address the threat posed by returning foreign terrorist fighters'.[30] These sentiments were echoed by the then Home Secretary, Theresa May, in relation to the CTS Bill:

The substance is right. The time is right. And the way in which it has been developed is right. It is not a knee-jerk response to a sudden perceived threat. It is a properly-considered, thought-through set of proposals that will help to keep us safe at a time of very significant danger. . . . *It is deliberately focused on practical measures that we can be confident will work.*[31]

This book analyses whether these claims of effectiveness are borne out in practice. In other words, whether the new and amended legislation—which the UK and Australian Governments claimed were a necessary addition to the counter-terrorism armoury of the State—have been effective in achieving their goals.

Notes

1 The following information is extracted from Robert Mendick et al., 'Security Services Missed Five Opportunities to Stop the Manchester Bomber', *The Telegraph*, 6 June 2017 <www.telegraph.co.uk/news/2017/05/24/security-services-missed-five-opportunities-stop-manchester/>. This and all of the other hyperlinks in this book were correct at 7 December 2017.
2 United Kingdom, *Parliamentary Debates*, House of Commons, 22 June 2017, vol. 626, col. 195 (Amber Rudd, Home Secretary).
3 David Anderson, 'Attacks in London and Manchester' (December 2017) 15–16.
4 This book uses the term 'Islamic State' to refer to the organisation variously known as ISIL (Islamic State in Iraq and the Levant), ISIS (Islamic State in Iraq and Syria or Islamic State in Iraq and al-Sham), and Daesh.
5 James Renwick, 'Sections 119.2 and 119.3 of the Criminal Code: Declared Areas' (September 2017) 5.
6 George Williams, 'Overreaction to Khayre's Crimes Exactly What Terrorists Seek', *Sydney Morning Herald*, 16 June 2017 <www.smh.com.au/comment/overreaction-to-khayres-crimes-exactly-what-terrorists-seek-20170616-gwsdgu.html>.
7 Robin Wright, 'Does the Manchester Attack Show the Islamic State's Strength or Weakness?', *The New Yorker*, 24 May 2017 <www.newyorker.com/news/news-desk/does-the-manchester-attack-show-the-islamic-states-strength-or-weakness>.
8 See Chapter 2 at 10–11, 19.

9 Rukmini Callimachi and Eric Schmitt, 'Manchester Bomber Met with ISIS Unit in Libya, Officials Say', *New York Times*, 3 June 2017 <www.nytimes.com/2017/06/03/world/middleeast/manchester-bombing-salman-abedi-islamic-state-libya.html>.

10 Ely Karmon, *New Trends in the Global Jihadi* (International Institute for Counter-Terrorism, 30 May 2017) <www.ict.org.il/Article/2021/new-trends-in-the-global-jihadi-offensive#gsc.tab=0>.

11 See Marcello Flores, 'Foreign Fighters Involvement in National and International Wars: A Historical Survey', in Andrea de Guttry, Francesca Capone, and Christophe Paulussen (eds), *Foreign Fighters Under International Law and Beyond* (The Hague: TMC Asser Press, 2016) 27; Tom Keatinge, 'Identifying Foreign Terrorist Fighters: The Role of Public-Private Partnership, Information Sharing and Financial Intelligence' (RUSI, 15 August 2015); David Malet, *Foreign Fighters: Transnational Identity in Civil Conflicts* (Oxford: Oxford University Press, 2013).

12 SC Res 2178, UN SCOR, 7272nd mtg, UN Doc S/RES/2178 (24 September 2014).

13 Ibid., 2.

14 Ibid., [6(b)].

15 Press Association, 'Woman Jailed for Trying to Take Her Children to Live in Syria Under ISIS', *Guardian*, 8 January 2016 <www.theguardian.com/uk-news/2016/jan/08/woman-jailed-five-years-children-syria>. For a discussion of the legislative responses to the challenges posed by the families of foreign terrorist fighters, see Chapter 4 at 90–1.

16 Ben Farmer and Josie Ensor, 'British Jihadi Brides Return Home After Being Widowed or Sent Back by Husbands Preparing Last ISIL Stand', *The Telegraph*, 22 May 2017 <www.telegraph.co.uk/news/2017/05/22/british-jihadi-brides-returning-home-widowed-sent-home-husbands/>.

17 Commonwealth, *Parliamentary Debates*, Senate, 24 September 2014, 6999 (George Brandis, Attorney-General).

18 Amber Rudd, 'Home Secretary Statement on Recent Terrorist Attacks' (Oral statement delivered to Parliament, London, 22 June 2017) <www.gov.uk/government/speeches/home-secretary-statement-on-recent-terrorist-attacks>.

19 Richard Barrett, *Foreign Fighters in Syria* (The Soufan Group, June 2014) 6.

20 The Soufan Group, *Foreign Fighters: An Updated Assessment of the Flow of Foreign Fighters into Syria and Iraq* (8 December 2015) 4. The International Centre for Counter-Terrorism at The Hague estimated in 2016 that foreign fighters have travelled to Syria from 104 countries: International Centre for Counter-Terrorism, *The Foreign Fighters Phenomenon in the European Union Profiles, Threats & Policies* (Research Paper, April 2016) 3.

21 US Department of State, 'Country Reports on Terrorism 2015' (Press Release, 2 June 2016) <https://2009-2017.state.gov/r/pa/prs/ps/2016/06/258013.htm>.

22 Prevention of Terrorism (Temporary Provisions) Act 1974 (UK). This was the first UK-wide piece of anti-terrorism legislation. An anti-terrorism law limited to the jurisdiction of Northern Ireland had been enacted one year earlier: Northern Ireland (Emergency Provisions) Act 1973 (UK).

23 See Laura K. Donohue, *Counter-Terrorist Law and Emergency Powers in the United Kingdom 1922–2000* (Dublin: Irish Academic Press, 2007) 207–58. See also Criminal Justice (Terrorism and Conspiracy) Act 1998 (UK). The Real IRA is a dissident offshoot of the IRA.

24 Anti-Terrorism, Crime and Security Act 2001 (UK).

25 Terrorism Act 2006 (UK).

26 Counter-Terrorism and Security Act 2015 (UK).

27 Kent Roach, *The 9/11 Effect: Comparative Counter-Terrorism* (Cambridge: Cambridge University Press, 2011).

28 Fiona de Londras, 'Governance Gaps in EU Counter-Terrorism: Implications for Democracy and Constitutionalism', in Fiona de Londras and Josephine Doody (eds), *The Impact, Legitimacy, and Effectiveness of EU Counter-Terrorism* (Abingdon: Routledge, 2015) 222.

29 Commonwealth, *Parliamentary Debates*, House of Representatives, 22 September 2014, 9958 (Tony Abbott, Prime Minister).

30 Commonwealth, *Parliamentary Debates*, Senate, 24 September 2014, 7002–3 (George Brandis, Attorney-General).

31 Theresa May, 'Home Secretary Theresa May on Counter-Terrorism' (Speech delivered at RUSI, London, 24 November 2014) <www.gov.uk/government/speeches/home-secretary-theresa-may-on-counter-terrorism> (emphasis added).

2 Criminal Justice System

2.1 Introduction

Acts of terrorism are essentially criminal in character. This is so in spite of the militarised rhetoric of the 'war on terror', which has been prominent in political discourse since the September 11 terrorist attacks. The importance of the criminal justice system in responding to terrorism has been highlighted by the Eminent Jurists Panel on Terrorism, Counter-terrorism and Human Rights of the International Commission of Jurists. It wrote in its 2009 report 'Assessing Damage, Urging Action': 'A well-operating criminal justice system will deter terrorists, disrupt terrorist networks, catch and punish those who commit crimes, and ensure that any innocent suspects mistakenly caught up in the law enforcement process are rapidly released'.[1] This chapter will evaluate whether the criminal law has achieved these outcomes in its application to one particular facet of the terrorist threat, namely, the foreign terrorist fighters phenomenon.

2.2 The Legislative Framework

There are a wide range of criminal offences in both Australia and the UK which could potentially be relied upon to prosecute foreign terrorist fighters and their supporters. Most obviously, there are the traditional criminal offences, for example, murder, and their inchoate counterparts. The latter include offences such as incitement to murder, conspiracy to murder, and attempted murder. Neither Australia nor the UK has, however, been content to rely upon generally applicable legislation in responding to terrorism. Instead, they have each enacted specific offences which reflect the particularly insidious nature of terrorism, both in terms of the underlying motivation of the offender as well as the grave harm which may result. The definition of terrorism upon which these offences hinge is similar in each jurisdiction. This is unsurprising given that the Australian definition in s 101 of the Criminal Code was 'largely reproduced' from that in s 1 of the Terrorism Act 2000

(TA 2000).[2] In particular, both definitions go beyond harm to the person to encapsulate serious damage to property and interference with an electronic system. They also include a requirement that the use or threat of action be done to advance a particular kind of cause (political, religious, and ideological in both jurisdictions, as well as racial in the UK).

There are also some broad similarities in the structure of the criminal regimes in the two jurisdictions. Both Australia and the UK criminalise preparatory acts, participation in the activities of a terrorist organisation and the financing of terrorism. In Australia, these offences have been consolidated in the Criminal Code, with the UN Charter Act also setting out two financing offences. The UK's legislative regime is more fragmented, but the bulk of the terrorism offences are contained in the TA 2000 and Terrorism Act 2006 (TA 2006). Each of the jurisdictions has also criminalised terrorism-related speech, that is, 'encouragement' of terrorism in the UK[3] and 'advocating' terrorism in Australia.[4] However, beyond these broad structural similarities, the more one burrows down into the detail of the terrorism offences in each jurisdiction, the more differences begin to appear. One of the most striking is that the UK does not have a substantive offence of terrorism, whereas engaging in a terrorist act is criminalised in Australia pursuant to s 101.1 of the Criminal Code.

Australia's first body of national anti-terrorism legislation, enacted immediately after the September 11 terrorist attacks, was heavily influenced by the TA 2000. After all, the UK had enacted numerous pieces of legislation throughout the twentieth century in response to terrorism in Northern Ireland.[5] However, the growing confidence of the Australian Federal Parliament, combined with its freedom from the constraints of a human rights framework like the Human Rights Act 1998 (HRA), has led to increasingly divergent legislation.[6] The differences have become particularly pronounced in the criminal justice responses of each jurisdiction to the threat posed by foreign terrorist fighters.

Most notably, in 2014, the Australian Federal Parliament introduced s 119.2 into the Criminal Code. This makes it an offence to enter, or remain in, an area in a foreign country which has been 'declared' by the Minister for Foreign Affairs.[7] An area may be declared where the Minister is satisfied that 'a listed terrorist organisation is engaging in a hostile activity in that area of the foreign country'.[8] To date, the only areas which have been declared by the Australian Government are the regions of Mosul in Iraq and Al-Raqqa in Syria.[9] This offence is particularly significant because its introduction was justified as 'enabl[ing] law enforcement agencies to bring to justice those Australians who have committed serious offences, including associating with, and fighting for, terrorist organisations overseas'.[10] However, the language of urgency surrounding its introduction may be contrasted with the failure to utilise this offence until December 2017.

The declared area offence forms part of a new Part 5.5 of the Criminal Code. This Part is modelled—albeit with some amendments to modernise the offences—upon the now repealed Foreign Incursions Act. In addition to the declared area offence, this Part criminalises engaging in a hostile activity in a foreign country and entry into a foreign country with the intention of engaging in hostile activities. Section 119.4 also contains several offences relating to preparations for incursions (whether by the offender or another person) into a foreign country. The Foreign Incursions Act dates back to the 1970s, well in advance of the emergence of the threat posed by foreign terrorist fighters in the Syrian and Iraqi conflicts. Nevertheless, there are two reasons why it forms a crucial part of the story told in this book. First, it is only in the context of the modern threat posed by foreign terrorist fighters that the foreign incursions offences have been acknowledged as a crucial part of Australia's anti-terrorism legislative framework. The Explanatory Memorandum to the Foreign Fighters Bill identified that the new Part 5.5 of the Criminal Code is 'designed to . . . respond to the significant threat to the safety and security of Australia and Australians posed by those who engage in foreign fighting or seek to do so'.[11] Second, as will be discussed in more detail below, the Australian authorities have relied heavily upon the foreign incursions offences to prosecute people involved in the Syrian and Iraqi conflicts, whether on the front line or in a supporting role.

By comparison with Australia, the UK Parliament has been relatively restrained in enacting new substantive criminal offences to address the foreign terrorist fighters phenomenon. For example, despite the shift away from Northern Irish terrorism towards international terrorism as the primary source of the threat, the Parliament has not regarded it as necessary to enact legislation which generally criminalises hostile activities committed in a foreign country. Its response has instead—as is explored in more detail in Chapters 3 and 4—emphasised civil and administrative mechanisms for responding to this modern iteration of the terrorist threat. This does not mean that there has been no reliance upon the criminal justice system in the UK to address the foreign terrorist fighters phenomenon. To the contrary, there have been a large number of prosecutions under pre-existing terrorism offences, such as for membership of a proscribed terrorist organisation,[12] providing or receiving terrorist training[13] and preparation for terrorist acts.[14]

2.3 Application of the Criminal Law

2.3.1 To Foreign Terrorist Fighters

The logical place to start any assessment of the operation of the criminal law in the context of the foreign terrorist fighters phenomenon is with those who have actually travelled overseas to join the Syrian and Iraqi conflicts. There are two fundamental challenges in attempting to rely upon the criminal justice system to minimise the threat which such individuals pose to national security. The first of these is legal in nature. To be able to prosecute a person for conduct engaged in overseas, the relevant terrorism offence must have extraterritorial operation. To date, this has not been an insurmountable problem in either Australia or the UK. In Australia, the individual and group-based terrorism offences in the Criminal Code have always applied regardless of whether or not 'the conduct constituting the alleged offence occurs in Australia' or 'a result of the conduct constituting the alleged offence occurs in Australia'.[15]

The granting of extraterritorial jurisdiction over the terrorism offences has been a slower and far more complex process in the UK. Nevertheless, the general trend in this country—as in many others across the world—has been towards the '[m]ore frequent assertion of extraterritorial jurisdiction. . . [as a] manifestation of the increased transnational complexity of antiterrorism law'.[16] In *R v F*, the Court of Appeal noted that '[i]t would be unrealistic to approach the terrorist legislation on the basis that Parliament envisaged that it should not apply to countries allied to us or to other members of the United Nations'.[17] Thus, the TA 2000 asserted extraterritorial jurisdiction over many of the offences contained therein, such as that of directing the activities of a terrorist organisation.[18] This Act also made it an offence to incite another person to commit an act of terrorism outside the UK.[19] The TA 2006 continued this trend. It provided in Schedule 17 that the offence of membership of a proscribed terrorist organisation in the TA 2000 applies to acts done outside the UK and, furthermore, to foreign nationals.

When introduced by the TA 2006, the offences of providing or receiving terrorist training[20] and encouraging terrorism[21] were given extraterritorial operation in part.[22] A person could be tried before the UK courts for making statements overseas, or providing or receiving training overseas where it was undertaken for the commission, preparation, or instigation of an offence under the 2005 Council of Europe Convention on the Prevention of Terrorism.[23] Most recently, and against the backdrop of the foreign terrorist fighters phenomenon, the UK Parliament adopted the Serious Crime Act 2015 (UK). Section 81 of this Act extended extraterritorial jurisdiction to the training offence in its entirety as well as to the offence of doing acts in preparation for terrorism in s 5 of the TA 2006.

It is notable that even where extraterritorial jurisdiction has not been asserted, there is nevertheless an alternative path that the authorities might take, namely, to prosecute a person for any acts engaged in prior to travelling to—or after returning home from—the conflict zones. This strategy has been used by the UK with respect to foreign terrorist fighters on a number of occasions, especially where the conduct concerned took place prior to the extension of extraterritorial jurisdiction to s 5. For example, according to the UK Government, the

> conviction of Mashudur Choudhury in May 2014 for engaging in conduct in preparation of terrorist acts . . . was based on activities which took place in the UK, and his prosecution would not have been possible if his preparatory activity had taken place solely outside the UK.[24]

The second challenge, which is practical rather than legal in nature, has played a significant role in the Australian context in particular. It is a truism that a person cannot be prosecuted for a criminal offence under domestic law unless they have returned, either voluntarily or as a result of coercion, to that country. In the UK, it is reported that just under half (or 400) of the estimated 850 people who have travelled to the conflict zones in Syria and Iraq have returned.[25] This does not mean that all of the returnees have been prosecuted. As will be discussed in more detail in the next section, it has frequently been the case that charges have not been laid either because the returnees entered the country undetected and the authorities remain in the dark as to their identities, or due to difficulties in collecting sufficient admissible evidence to prove their guilt to the criminal standard of beyond a reasonable doubt.

In Australia, a significant number of arrest warrants have been issued by the authorities for individuals who have travelled to Syria or Iraq. The precise number of warrants and the names of the majority of those concerned are not a matter of public record. However, as at 18 November 2015, the Australian Federal Police (AFP) stated that 11 arrest warrants had been issued for Australians involved in the Syrian conflict.[26] *The Australian* newspaper reported in July 2017 that the AFP had obtained arrest warrants for 18 Australian foreign terrorist fighters in Syria and Iraq.[27] The vast majority remain outstanding because the subjects of these warrants have not returned to Australia. To date, only 40 Australians have returned from the conflict zones and, of those, 35 re-entered the country prior to the declaration of a caliphate by Islamic State.[28] In other words, 'they were, in the main, Australian citizens who were involved in the civil war in Syria and were more interested in the internecine conflict than in targeting what [the Director-General] . . . describe[d] as the West'.[29]

It is statistically more likely that an Australian foreign terrorist fighter will be killed in the conflict zones than that they will return to domestic soil. For example, of the six people subject to an arrest warrant who have been named by the authorities, three—Khaled Sharrouf, Mohamed Elomar, and Mohammad Ali Bayalei—are confirmed to have died.[30] In May 2017, the Director-General of Security, Duncan Lewis, estimated that at least 64—and possibly as many as 76—Australians had been killed in the Syrian and Iraqi conflicts.[31] In addition to death in the conflict zones, there are two other significant reasons why a person might not return to Australia. One is the combined effect of Australia's geographical distance from the conflict zones and its tight controls on immigration. Lewis gave evidence to a Senate Estimates Hearing in May 2017 that:

> Australian borders are very strong, so if one of these fighters tries to get back into Australia, they will be detected upon return and they will then face whatever the consequences of the law are. The full force of the law will be applied to them. That is the reason why we think that there will be fewer returning.[32]

This was reiterated by the Attorney-General, George Brandis. He stated on 27 March 2017 that 'of the 100 Australians currently remaining in the conflict zone', it was likely 'only a small number may attempt to return to Australia' in the future.[33] For example, Tareq Kamleh—also the subject of an outstanding arrest warrant—has indicated that he has no intention of ever returning to Australia.[34]

In circumstances where a foreign terrorist fighter does not return to Australia voluntarily, another factor comes into play. This refers to the possibility of needing to rely upon foreign authorities, especially Turkey given its close proximity to Syria, to intercept, detain, and extradite individuals to Australia. Such was the case in respect of Neil Prakesh, for whom an arrest warrant was issued in August 2015. After travelling to Syria in September 2013, Prakesh became a leading Islamic State recruiter and appeared in several propaganda videos. He was detained by immigration authorities in November 2016 after he attempted to cross the border into Turkey. At the time of writing— more than a year later—Australia has not yet been successful in negotiating his return, despite the existence of a bilateral extradition treaty between the countries.[35]

2.3.2 To Returned Foreign Terrorist Fighters

As is discussed in Chapter 4, both Australia and the UK have enacted measures for the purpose of overseeing and controlling the movements of foreign terrorist fighters and their supporters. Some of these measures, like passport suspensions and cancellations, have been effectively utilised in Australia to disrupt the foreign travel plans of potential fighters. This has been made possible by the significantly lower number of Australian foreign terrorist fighters than their UK counterparts. At its highest point in September 2014, official estimates of the number of Australian foreign terrorist fighters were in the order of 140.[36] This number has since decreased to around 100.[37] These figures are dwarfed by those in the UK. As mentioned above, approximately 850 people from the UK are believed to have travelled to fight with, or provide support to, Islamic State, Al-Qaida, and their affiliates.[38] In light of those figures, it is unsurprising that the UK authorities have been unable to identify every foreign terrorist fighter either upon leaving the country or returning. This has had significant implications for the efficacy of the criminal law as a means of addressing the national security risk posed by returned foreign terrorist fighters. Given the very different statistical profiles of Australia and the UK, and the distinct issues which flow from these, the issues in each jurisdiction will be discussed in turn below.

2.3.2.1 *Australia*

Only a small number of individuals have returned to Australia after fighting in the Syrian and Iraqi conflicts. Of those, the vast majority were involved in the conflicts prior to the Islamification of the Syrian opposition movement and are therefore not regarded as posing a significant threat to national security. There are, of course, some exceptions. For example, seven men were recruited by Hamdi Alqudsi to travel to Syria to join Jabhat al-Nusra in mid-2013.[39] One of those men, Mehmet Biber, returned to Australia in January 2014 and—almost three years later—was charged with foreign incursions offences in relation to his own travel as well as actively supporting others to travel to the conflict zones.[40]

Of the individuals involved in the Syrian and Iraqi conflicts in the period since the declaration of a caliphate by Islamic State, the names of four returnees have been disclosed by the authorities: George Khamis, Matthew Gardiner, Adam Brookman and Ashley Dyball. All of these men were investigated by the authorities after re-entering Australia; however, ultimately only one was charged. Despite the small sample size, this statistic would appear to suggest that the vast majority of people who return to Australia are unlikely to be prosecuted. There are three reasons for this.

First, foreign terrorist fighters who *choose* to return to Australia from these conflict zones will often have opposed—rather than supported—Islamic State.[41] Gardiner and Dyball, for example, were suspected of fighting with the YPG in Syria against Islamic State.[42] Similarly, Khamis allegedly joined an Assyrian militia group, Dwekh Nawsha, fighting against the Iraqi branch of Islamic State.[43] Brookman is an outlier in this regard, being the only one of the returnees to have travelled to the conflict zones to support Islamic State. Given this, it is unsurprising that he was the only one of the four men to be prosecuted for terrorism. Just days after his return to Australia in July 2015, he was charged with knowingly providing support to a terrorist organisation by having undertaken guard duty and reconnaissance for Islamic State whilst in Syria.[44] It is not only the mere fact of desiring to return home to Australia which makes Brookman exceptional. It is well known that Islamic State 'doesn't let fighters abandon the group without consequence'.[45] Brookman was extremely unusual in that he successfully escaped from Islamic State by crossing the border into Turkey, whereupon he surrendered to the authorities and was back on Australian soil three days later.

The second reason why prosecutions of returned foreign terrorist fighters are statistically unlikely is that those who return will only be able to do so after reaching an agreement with the Australian authorities. For those foreign terrorist fighters whose names are known to the authorities—in which case it is almost certain that their Australian passports will have been cancelled or at least suspended—arrangements will need to be made through the Department of Foreign Affairs for alternative documentation to enable their return to Australia. This is not impossible, but at the very least represents an 'administrative hurdle'.[46] For example, Kurdish journalist, Renas Lelikan, was not provided with temporary travel documents to enable him to return to Australia until after he had already spent nine months in an Iraqi refugee camp.[47]

Although not the case with Lelikan, it is possible that a person would only voluntarily return to Australia after being guaranteed that they would not face prosecution. The benefits of such an arrangement to the individual returnee are self-evident. More difficult to comprehend, however, are any benefits to national security and thus why the Australian authorities might be willing to offer such a guarantee. Nevertheless, there is now a substantial body of academic scholarship which concludes that disillusioned foreign terrorist fighters are uniquely placed to offer a counter-narrative to the propaganda of Islamic State for the purpose of curbing the spread of extremist ideology and deradicalising particular individuals. Bob De Graaff writes that

> The best champions for . . . a counter-narrative will not be the authorities in the West, just as a teacher or a police officer are not the most suitable persons to keep youths from starting to use drugs or commit crime. . . . [I]n the war of words against Islamic State the persons most suited to propagate the message are disillusioned jihadists who have returned to their countries of origin in the West. These recanters are proof *par excellence* that the Islamic State is not as ideal as it looked to some at first sight.[48]

The third reason revolves around the inherently political character of decision-making in the anti-terrorism context. The former Prime Minister, Tony Abbott, warned in May 2015 that any foreign terrorist fighter who attempted to return to Australia would be prosecuted to the full extent of the law because 'a crime is a crime is a crime'.[49] Similar statements have been made by the Attorney-General, George Brandis:

> If you fight illegally in overseas conflicts, you face up to life in prison upon your return to Australia. We know there are some Australians who think they've made the right choice in becoming involved in overseas conflicts, but that choice only adds to the suffering in Syria and Iraq and it's putting those Australians and others in mortal danger.[50]

Based upon official statements such as these, Tim Legrand reached the conclusion that 'government policy is unambiguous: without exception, those who have supported IS or other illegal groups in proscribed areas in the Middle East will be arrested and prosecuted if they attempt to return to Australia'.[51] This even-handed approach has obvious merit. Shanahan, for example, has emphasised that '[t]he punitive element needs to be done and seen to be done otherwise the Muslim community will point out the inconsistency of applying the law to one side and not the other'.[52] On the other hand, however, it ignores the politics of the situation, namely, that Australia has provided both physical and moral support to particular opponents of Islamic State.[53] It would be difficult to explain the decision to prosecute a person for joining an organisation which shares the same political goals as Australia and in circumstances where the Australian Government has chosen to explicitly or implicitly endorse its violent tactics. An infamous example of this—albeit in the UK context—was the withdrawal of terrorism charges against Bherlin Gildo for his involvement with the Free Syrian Army. He was facing trial for attending a place used for terrorist training and training for terrorism, however, his legal counsel told the court:

> If it is the case that HM government was actively involved in supporting armed resistance to the Assad regime at a time when the defendant was present in Syria and himself participating in such resistance it would be unconscionable to allow the prosecution to continue.[54]

In withdrawing the charges on the basis that '[m]any matters were raised we did not know at the outset', the prosecution seems to have acquiesced.[55]

Andrew Zammit builds upon this by suggesting that politics is not the only consideration at play. Rather, there is a substantive difference between the categories of foreign terrorist fighters. He argues that '[n]ot all foreign terrorist fighters are the same—there are degrees of seriousness, and fighting for a proscribed terrorist organisation is a more serious crime than fighting against one'.[56] Periodic attempts have been made to incorporate a distinction along these lines into Australia's anti-terrorism legislative regime. For example, in the aftermath of the death of YPG fighter, Jamie Bright, in Syria in May 2016, the former Independent National Security Legislation Monitor (INSLM), Bret Walker, recommended the introduction of a legislative framework whereby the executive branch of government could formally earmark activities during a particular foreign conflict as legitimate or illegitimate.[57] Whilst still maintaining a degree of flexibility, this framework would be preferable to what he described as the current 'wink-and-a-nod' approach whereby the criminal law was inconsistently enforced.[58] This recommendation has not, however, been adopted by the Australian Federal Parliament. The argument made by Zammit about the substantive difference between the categories of foreign terrorist fighters is therefore relevant only to the extent that it is applied by intelligence agencies, their law enforcement counterparts, and prosecutors as part of their decision-making processes.[59]

The above discussion is directed at the likelihood of returned foreign terrorist fighters being charged with terrorism offences in the first instance. This is not, however, the only limitation upon the effectiveness of the criminal law in combatting this manifestation of the threat of terrorism. The delay of almost three years between the return of Mehmet Biber to Australia and the laying of charges highlights the often insurmountable difficulties in gathering sufficient admissible evidence to prove a returnee's activities to the criminal standard of beyond a reasonable doubt. Walker commented in his 2014 Annual Report that 'the problem of overseas evidence is peculiarly challenging for the prosecution of terrorist offenders'.[60] There is no single (or simple) reason for this. Instead, there are a multitude of intersecting practical and evidentiary issues. One is how to gather information about the activities of an individual or organisation overseas, especially in countries in a state of civil war. Another is the willingness of foreign intelligence agencies to give evidence in open court. Finally, there is the need to comply—and prove compliance—with the rules of evidence so far as the methods of collection of information are concerned. As the AFP informed Walker in March 2014:

> The current situation in Syria is complicated by the fact that the Assad Government controls certain sections of the country, where rival opposition groups hold quasi-control over other sections of the State. Gaining police-to-police assistance in such scenarios is almost impossible. Further it is unlikely that evidence gathered by government or quasi-government forces would meet the high evidentiary threshold requirements under Australian law.[61]

Two steps have been taken by the Australian Federal Parliament in response to these challenges. First, the Foreign Fighters Act introduced into the Criminal Code the offence of intentionally entering, or remaining in, a declared area in a foreign country where the person knows, or should know, that the area is a declared area.[62] This offence carries a maximum penalty of ten years imprisonment. Whilst this offence was ostensibly aimed at preventing Australians from travelling to dangerous regions and potentially returning with the mindset and capability to conduct a domestic terrorist attack, it also had the effect of making it significantly easier to establish criminality. This is because it criminalised the mere act of travelling to a declared area without also requiring proof of an intention to engage in hostile activities or terrorism. The reality is that motivation is rarely made an element of criminal offences. This is, at least in part, because of the difficulties in proving what a person thought, as opposed to what they said or did. Such difficulties are considerable even where that person remains at all times on domestic soil and thus the authorities are able to gather information by way of human surveillance and telecommunications interceptions. Where the relevant conduct occurs overseas and the authorities do not have these tools at their disposal, the difficulties are virtually insurmountable.

In addition to amending the substantive criminal law, Walker recommended a range of legislative amendments to remedy the situation whereby 'not merely prosecutions but also investigations are presently stillborn on account of problems of foreign evidence'.[63] One of the most significant was the amendment of the Foreign Evidence Act to bestow greater discretion upon judges to admit foreign material at the same time as maintaining existing protections of the defendant's right to a fair trial.[64] The Foreign Fighters Act removed the limitation that only foreign evidence obtained through a formal government-to-government request was admissible. Instead, it is now permissible for evidence obtained through informal cooperation between Australia and overseas agencies to be admitted in criminal proceedings. The small number of returnees—and the even smaller number of charges laid against them—means that it is not yet possible to determine whether the legislative amendments have increased the conviction rate in terrorism-related prosecutions.

2.3.2.2 UK

Only a very small proportion of returned foreign terrorist fighters have been prosecuted in the UK. This is not—as in Australia—because of the minimal number of returnees, but rather quite the opposite. Official estimates are that around 400 foreign terrorist fighters have returned to the UK.[65] Some experts suggest that the number of returnees could be as high as 800 to 1,000 given the possibility of foreign terrorist fighters re-entering the country undetected.[66] The sheer number of returnees, as well as the proliferation of Islamic State supporters on domestic soil, means that the resources of immigration, law enforcement, and intelligence agencies have been stretched thin. In the House of Lords in April 2016, Lord Keen of Elie stated that

> The Crown Prosecution Service has successfully prosecuted 35 cases involving 54 defendants who have returned to the UK and are suspected of having fought in Syria and/or Iraq. [In other words, around one in eight returnees have been convicted.] It currently has 13 such ongoing prosecutions involving 30 defendants. The Public Prosecution Service Northern Ireland (PPSNI) is also dealing with one ongoing Syria-related prosecution.[67]

In the place of more up-to-date statements being released by the UK authorities, the best source of information is the BBC Jihadist Database.[68] In July 2017, the BBC stated that of the 109 people who had been convicted of terrorism offences relating to the Syrian and Iraqi conflicts since 2014, less than 15 percent (or 16 people) had been to Syria or Iraq.[69] This again indicates that only a very small proportion of returned foreign terrorist fighters have been prosecuted—let alone convicted—of criminal offences.

Those who have been prosecuted upon their return to the UK have been charged with a variety of ordinary criminal offences, especially those relating to firearms as well as terrorism offences. On the basis of publicly available information, it would appear that no returnees have yet been prosecuted specifically for involvement in combat in Syria or Iraq. There have been instances in which the prosecution has pointed to evidence of armed activity overseas as evidence of other offences and the motivation underpinning them. For example, the evidence against Imran Mohammed Khawaja included photographs of him posing with child soldiers in Syria and holding severed heads. His activities were described by the Deputy Head of Counter-Terrorism at the Crown Prosecution Service, Deborah Walsh, as 'one of the most appalling examples of violent extremism that I have seen committed by British jihadis returning from Syria'.[70] Nevertheless, even in that case, the prosecution did not charge Khawaja with an offence that would have required proof to the criminal standard of beyond a reasonable doubt of involvement in combat in Syria, such as murder or offences under the Explosive Substances Act 1883 (UK). This would seem to have been a wise decision in light of the conclusion subsequently reached by the sentencing judge that the video and photographic evidence against Khawaja was 'equally open to the inference, that whilst being in extremely close proximity to one of the combat zones and assisting those who had returned from the front line, [he] did not actually take part in the fighting itself'.[71] Recent assertions made by parliamentarians that returned foreign terrorist fighters should be charged with treason[72] or, in the alternative, war crimes or genocide, would face even more significant difficulties in terms of proof.[73]

The vast majority of prosecutions of returned foreign terrorist fighters in the UK have relied upon offences which capture conduct in advance of, or in some way removed from, the commission of a terrorist act. The reliance upon preparatory offences can be attributed to the significant difficulties in gathering evidence about conduct overseas and the defendant's motivation for engaging in that conduct. For example, after returning from a trip to Syria in October 2014, Mustafa Abdullah was charged not in relation to the activities he engaged in abroad, but rather files found on his phone and computer with respect to weapons instruction and guerrilla warfare.[74] He was ultimately convicted by a jury of 13 counts of possessing a terrorist document or article. Mohammed Uddin pleaded guilty to the same charge as well as an additional one of preparing for acts of terrorism.[75] The prosecution case was that he had travelled to Syria in November 2014 with the intention of joining Islamic State and engaging in combat. However, he crossed the border back into Turkey just a month later. Upon flying into Gatwick Airport in late December 2014, Uddin was stopped by counter-terrorism officers. Subsequent investigations revealed a significant amount of extremist material in Uddin's possession and, furthermore, that he had meticulously planned his travel to Syria to ensure that he was not detected by the authorities.

The ability of the prosecution to rely solely upon conduct on domestic soil depends, of course, on there being a clear pattern of preparatory behaviour prior to the travel to Syria (as in the case of Uddin) or inculpatory evidence found in the defendant's possession upon their return (as in the cases of both Abdullah and Uddin). In some instances, however, these are either not present or are insufficient for the purposes of a criminal trial. Such was the situation with respect to Tareena Shakil. Although she spent several weeks preparing to travel overseas, including talking to two key British women inside Islamic State, the crucial evidence against Shakil were her posts on social media whilst in Syria. These included a photograph of her toddler son next to an AK47 with the name 'Abu Jihad al-Britani' superimposed over the top as well as regular Tweets professing her support for Islamic State.[76] In spite of this evidence, the case against Shakil was not without its challenges. The prosecution chose to charge Shakil with not only encouraging terrorism,[77] but also belonging to a proscribed organisation.[78] Before taking part in any military training, male foreign terrorist fighters are required to swear an oath of allegiance to Islamic State.[79] These requirements do not, however, apply to women. This created difficulties in terms of establishing the element of 'belonging'. There was no evidence that Shakil did—at least in so far as that term refers to formal membership—belong to Islamic State. The jury's finding of guilt on both counts implies that it took a broader approach to this concept. Similarly, in sentencing Shakil to six years imprisonment, Judge Inman stated that:

> Your role as a woman in Isis was different to that of a man but you embraced it and were willing to support those in Raqqa, and potentially those outside, to come and play their role in providing fighters of the future and were willing, shamelessly, to allow your son to be photographed in terms that could only be taken as a fighter of the future.[80]

In addition to the preparatory offences, other offences which have been relied upon in the context of returned foreign terrorist fighters are those of attending a place used for terrorist training and training for terrorism. There have been several successful prosecutions under these offences. Imran Mohammed Khawaja, for example, pleaded guilty to a number of terrorism offences, including undertaking training for terrorism in the use of firearms in Syria between March and June 2014.[81] However, the difficulties in gathering evidence about activities overseas—even the mere act of attendance at a terrorist training camp—means that an alternative approach has sometimes had to be taken. Rather than charging brothers Hamza and Mohommod Nawaz with training for terrorism per se, the prosecution chose the safer option of relying upon the inchoate offence of conspiracy to attend a place used for terrorist training.[82] The caution displayed by the prosecution is particularly noteworthy given the large body of inculpatory evidence, including photographs of the daily schedule at the training camp, which was found in the Nawaz brothers' possession when they were detained. Indeed, in his sentencing judgement after guilty pleas were entered by both men, Judge Moss stated that

> [i]t is clear from the evidence from mobile phones that you had both been in a camp in Syria used for terrorist training. The evidence shows you were there for jihad, or holy war, and wanted to join an extremist group.[83]

For the reasons outlined in Chapter 1, the foreign terrorist fighters phenomenon is not homogenous. It is therefore important to give some attention—as has already been done above with regard to the Australian situation—to the treatment of returned anti-Islamic State fighters by the UK authorities. In December 2016, Josh Walker became the first such returnee to be charged with terrorism offences.[84] Shilan Ozcelik had previously been convicted and sentenced to a term of two years imprisonment for travelling to Belgium with the intention of going on from there to join the YPJ.[85] However, because she was ultimately unable or unwilling to enter Syria, she is more accurately characterised as the first UK citizen to be charged and convicted for *attempting* to join the campaign against Islamic State. The basis upon which the authorities initially questioned Walker and searched his property was that he had spent six months fighting with the YPG in Syria. He was initially charged with preparatory offences relating to these activities; however, this charge was withdrawn by the authorities. He subsequently faced a separate charge for possession of a partial copy of the infamous *The Anarchist Cookbook* which had been discovered by the authorities during the search.[86] On its face, such a charge would appear to be completely unrelated to Walker's admission that he had participated in the conflict in Syria. What is striking, however, is that the *Cookbook* is freely available on the internet, and more than 2 million copies have been sold. This gives rise to some doubt as to the real reason why Walker, but not any of the tens, hundreds, or even thousands of other owners of the *Cookbook* in the UK, was charged in relation to its possession. In any event, in late October 2017, he was acquitted of the possession offence.[87]

Viewed holistically, the approach taken by the UK authorities to returned anti-Islamic State fighters has been inconsistent and heavily dependent upon the political climate at the relevant point in time. During a debate in the UK Parliament six months prior to Walker's arrest, Conservative parliamentarian, Robert Jenrick, stated:

> Of the 20 [returned anti-Islamic State fighters] I have spoken with or their families, two were arrested under the Terrorism Act [namely, Aiden Aslen and Joe Robinson]; four were questioned, but not arrested; 14 came and went at will, unquestioned, three of whom [including Macer Giford] have been on a second or third tour of duty overseas.[88]

Just as in Australia, debates are ongoing in the UK as to whether there is a moral distinction between combat on behalf of Islamic State as compared to its opponents. However, to date, law enforcement and intelligence agencies have refused to formally draw any such distinction. It is only where embarrassment to the authorities might result from evidence given during trial that prosecutions have been withdrawn. Such was the case in relation to Bherlin Gildo discussed above. The other institution involved in the criminal justice system—the courts—has similarly refused to take the identity and ideology of the particular organisation into account. In relation to the prosecution of Yusuf Sarwar and Mohammed Ahmed, who, unlike Gildo, pleaded guilty to terrorism offences, defence counsel submitted to the court that their involvement with the Free Syria Army, a coalition of anti-Assad groups which had been supported and even supplied by Western countries, should be taken into account in sentencing.[89] This was rejected by the trial judge (and the Court of Appeal) on the basis that it would amount to 'a consideration of the policies of Her Majesty's Government' and '[t]o adopt such an approach would necessitate the court having to consider fine political arguments in a situation which is inherently fluid and uncertain, and where loyalties are not fixed or clear-cut'.[90] All that was relevant for the purposes of sentencing was that the conduct 'clearly came within the ambit of terrorism'.[91]

2.3.3 To Attempted Foreign Terrorist Fighters

The most effective use of the criminal law in both Australia and the UK has unsurprisingly been in respect of those individuals who have—at all relevant times—remained on domestic soil. They fall into two broad categories. First, individuals who have attempted unsuccessfully to travel overseas to support terrorist organisations involved in the Syrian and Iraqi conflicts. The other category—which will be discussed in the next section below—captures a disparate range of individuals and groups that either sympathise with (to put it in ideological terms) or support (in a practical sense) Islamic State, its goals and activities.

To date, around 15 individuals have been arrested in Australia for attempting to travel overseas to fight in the Syrian and Iraqi conflict zones. It is possible to make a relatively accurate calculation here because of the small numbers involved (at least in comparison with the flow of foreign terrorist fighters from other countries, especially those in western Europe). Similar comprehensive figures have not been released by the UK authorities. However, it is nevertheless possible to identify a number of individual cases and to draw themes from these about the operation of the criminal justice system with regard to attempted foreign terrorist fighters.

The first person in Australia to be caught in the act of attempting to travel overseas to fight in the Syrian and Iraqi conflicts was Amin Mohamed, a New Zealand national resident in Australia. Mohamed was stopped at Brisbane Airport in September 2013 and refused entry to a flight to Istanbul. As with the vast majority of attempted foreign terrorist fighters in Australia since then, Mohamed was charged with doing an act preparatory to an incursion into a foreign State with the intention to engage in hostile activity in that State, that is, foreign incursions offences under the Foreign Incursions Act (until 2014) or the Criminal Code (since 2014). Mohamed was assisted and advised in his travel plans by Hamdi Alqudsi, who was convicted in 2016 of offences relating to his role as a leading Islamic State recruiter.[92] Although the foreign incursions offences do not hinge upon the definition of terrorism outlined earlier in this chapter, there is nevertheless a motivational element which comes into play. Indeed, the only issue at trial was whether the prosecution could prove to the criminal standard of beyond a reasonable doubt that Mohamed's intention in going to Syria was to engage in hostile activity.[93] In convicting him, the jury concluded—largely on the basis of

intercepted telephone conversations between the defendant and Alqudsi—
that he intended to go to the 'front line' and, if necessary, 'be a martyr'.[94]

Subsequently, in May 2014, Fatima Elomar—the Australian wife of
Islamic State foreign terrorist fighter, Mohamed Elomar—was arrested as
she was about to board a flight to Malaysia with her four children. Cash,
medical supplies, and other items requested by her husband were found in
her possession at the time.[95] Probably the most high-profile arrest to date was
that of Jamie Williams in July 2015. Six months prior, Williams attempted
to travel to the northern Iraqi city of Sulaymaniyah to fight with the YPG
against Islamic State.[96]

The differing outcomes in these three completed cases reinforce the point
made above about the inherently political nature of prosecuting foreign terrorist fighters. Mohamed was convicted in October 2015 and sentenced to a
term of imprisonment of five years and six months. Elomar pleaded guilty to
terrorism-related offences, and a suspended jail term was imposed. In contrast, the Attorney-General, George Brandis, instructed the Commonwealth
Director of Public Prosecutions not to continue with the case against Williams.[97] No explanation was given; instead, a spokesman for the Attorney-
General simply stated that he 'has a broad discretion and is able to take into
account a number of factors'.[98] The same trend has been apparent in the UK.
In April 2016, three former YPG fighters—Joshua Molloy, Joe Akerman,
and Jac Holmes—were arrested for attempting to illegally cross the border
into Iraq.[99] After a week in detention and considerable pressure upon Iraqi
authorities from the British Consulate, the three men were released. Molloy
subsequently returned to the UK without facing charges.

In the absence of any equivalent to the foreign incursions offences in the
UK, the authorities in that jurisdiction have been forced to rely upon other
terrorism offences. Of particular note in this regard is the offence of preparing for acts of terrorism.[100] The underlying conduct in respect of which
attempted foreign terrorist fighters have been charged has unsurprisingly
included travelling to countries which border Syria and Iraq. Yahya Rashid,
for example, used a student loan to fund the travel of himself and four
friends to an Islamic State safe house on the Turkish border.[101] He ultimately
had a change of heart and returned voluntarily to the UK. Alex Nash also
travelled to Turkey but—in contrast to Rashid—was thereupon deported
back to the UK.[102]

However, the scope of the offence of preparing for acts of terrorism
extends considerably further to capture instances where the planning is far
less progressed. UK citizens and residents have been prosecuted for speaking
to members of Islamic State about the possibility of travel, researching travel
plans, and buying airline tickets. The evidence against Zakariya Ashiq, for

example, included WhatsApp recordings describing the efforts he made to join three friends fighting in Syria as he travelled across Europe.[103] Whilst the preparatory offence was designed to capture such activities, there are nevertheless challenges inherent in charging people for conduct so far removed from the commission of a terrorist act. In particular, the earlier the point in time at which a person is charged, the more difficult it will be to prove their ultimate goal. This is so regardless of whether they are prosecuted under anti-terrorism legislation in the UK, anti-terrorism legislation in Australia or the foreign incursions regime.

This chapter has already observed the limited extent to which the authorities have been able to identify those who travel overseas for the purpose of participating in the Syrian and Iraqi conflicts as well as those who subsequently seek to return. A similar point might be made, but to an even greater extent, in respect of those who unsuccessfully attempt to join those conflicts. The reality is that individuals will only come to the attention of the authorities where they have taken practical steps to travel to Syria or Iraq and, furthermore, the purpose of travel has been communicated in some way to the authorities. The latter may occur through tip-offs from family or friends,[104] or where the individual outlines their plans in intercepted conversations or directly to an undercover officer.[105] In the UK, many individuals have been arrested prior to boarding an international flight[106] or crossing the English Channel at Dover.[107] Yet more Britons have been stopped in other countries en route to Syria and returned to the UK whereupon they have been arrested. The geographical isolation of Australia, as well as the strictness of its border controls, means that oftentimes more extreme measures need to be taken by attempted foreign terrorist fighters. In a particularly bizarre instance, five men were arrested in May 2016 after towing a boat from Melbourne to far north Queensland. The authorities alleged that they were planning to go by boat to Indonesia and from there travel through the Philippines to Syria to join Islamic State.[108] The trial is due to commence in January 2018.

In addition to the limitations of the criminal justice system revealed by the above discussion, the reality is that the majority of attempted foreign terrorist fighters—as with foreign terrorist fighters themselves—will quite simply go undetected. Their plans will come to an end (whether voluntarily or thwarted by external factors), or they will travel overseas without the authorities ever being aware. Most infamously, the perpetrator of the London Bridge terrorist attack, Khuram Butt, was prevented from travelling to Syria to fight for Islamic State when his family confiscated his passport.[109] The authorities only appear to have become aware of this information after the attack was committed and further investigations into his background were undertaken.

2.3.4 *To Sympathisers on Domestic Soil*

At first glance, it might seem a stretch to include sympathisers on domestic soil in a discussion about the foreign terrorist fighters phenomenon. However, those who participate or attempt to participate in the Syrian and Iraqi conflicts do not do so in a vacuum. As the example of Hamdi Alqudsi discussed above demonstrates, their conduct is supported by extensive networks of individuals and organisations on domestic soil. The activities undertaken by these networks are regarded by the authorities as 'just as criminal and just as dangerous' as that of actually fighting with Islamic State.[110] As Judge Dodgson stated in sentencing Mustakim Jaman in the UK for assisting several people to travel to Syria:

> This was the celebration of terrorist acts and you . . . played an important part in providing moral support and on occasions engaging in acts, which were done with the intention of assisting others to engage in acts of terrorism. . . . It is right that you did not go to fight, but you were the drumbeat in the background, providing support for those who had gone and encouragement to those who might.[111]

On 25 May 2017, the Australian Director-General of Security, Duncan Lewis, estimated that there are 'around 200 people in Australia that are being investigated for providing support to individuals and groups involved in the Syria-Iraq conflict, including through funding and facilitation or seeking to travel there'.[112] Shortly after the bombing of the Ariana Grande concert in Manchester, the UK authorities revealed that more than 3,000 people were the subject of active terrorism-related investigations.[113] No information has been provided as to the percentage of those people whose activities are connected with the Syrian and Iraqi conflicts. However, it is safe to assume that this would be a significant proportion given that the number of persons arrested for *international* terrorism (as opposed to other categories such as domestic terrorism) in the year ending June 2017 was 294 (an increase of 60 percent on the previous year) and, furthermore, international terrorism accounted for 78 percent of all terrorism arrests that year.[114]

The activities in which these individuals have been involved can be divided into three rough categories: first, providing funds or other forms of material support to either an individual foreign terrorist fighter or the organisation with which they are involved; second, dissemination of propaganda on behalf of that organisation; and third, recruitment of foreign terrorist fighters. The latter two categories overlap in so far as one of the main purposes of Islamic State propaganda is to maximise support for the organisation, including the human resources at its disposal. Nicknamed the 'Twitter Terrorist' by the media, Alaa

Abdullah Esayed was convicted of terrorism offences under UK law in relation to more than 45,000 tweets expressing support for Islamic State. In sentencing her to three and a half years imprisonment, Judge Wide stated that

[t]he material you were disseminating encouraged young men to go and fight and . . . to encourage women to go to support them and indeed to bring up their children in the belief that it is their duty to take up arms to wage violent jihad and embrace martyrdom.[115]

The absence in the UK of a specific offence of recruitment means that there has been an additional degree of overlap between the second and third categories above. Recruiters have often faced the same charges as individuals involved in propaganda-related activities, namely, encouragement of terrorism,[116] dissemination of terrorist publications,[117] and inviting support for a proscribed organisation.[118] For example, Abdul Mohammed Kahar was charged with the last of these offences in relation to conversations in which he urged his nephew, brother-in-law, and friend to join Islamic State.[119] The Court of Appeal noted that this 'was serious offending of its type, given his persistence in attempting to persuade others to join Islamic State and fight for them or to join in their terrorism'.[120] Where the relevant activities are not captured by one of these specific offences, the prosecution has instead (or also) relied upon the offence of doing acts in preparation for terrorism. This catch-all offence has similarly been relied upon in the context of fundraising and other forms of material support associated with the Syrian and Iraqi conflicts. This is in addition to the specific offence of funding terrorism in s 17 of the TA 2000.

Returning to the category of propaganda-related activities, this has been by far the most common basis for charges against sympathisers located in the UK. This is in keeping with Islamic State's prolific use of the internet, and social media in particular, as a tool for radicalisation.[121] Thus, any person in the UK who sympathises with the organisation has the potential to become a 'keyboard warrior'. In relation to the investigation and subsequent prosecution of Samata Ullah for making large quantities of extremist material and instructional videos available to Islamic State supporters worldwide, the Counter-Terrorism Commander of the Metropolitan Police, Dean Hayden, stated:

Just because Ullah's activity was in the virtual world, we never underestimated how dangerous [it] was. . . . This is just the sort of information that may have helped people involved in planning devastating, low technical level, attacks on crowded places.[122]

The Australian authorities have not placed the same emphasis upon stemming the flow of Islamic State propaganda. In spite of the Foreign Fighters Act making it an offence to advocate—defined as counselling, promoting, encouraging, or urging—terrorism, this offence has not yet been relied on in the context of the foreign terrorist fighters phenomenon.[123] Instead, the Australian authorities have held off on laying charges until concrete action has been taken by the individual or group. For example, Hassan El Sabsabi was not arrested until just before he was due to transfer $12,000 to an unknown American man to enable him to travel to Syria. This is despite him previously using social media to express his support for Islamic State, such as by 'liking' images of dead soldiers and posting statements such as '[m]ay Allah destroy the shia and Alawi fighting the Muslims, these are the devils in the form of human beings'.[124]

In addition to the extensive fundraising, recruitment, and propaganda-related activities engaged in on domestic soil, there is a further reason why it is important to consider domestic sympathisers as part of the foreign terrorist fighters phenomenon. In recent years in both Australia and the UK, there has been a significant number of terrorist plots and attacks inspired by Islamic State. On 25 May 2017, the Australian Director-General of Security estimated that there had been four terrorist attacks on Australian soil since the declaration of a caliphate by Islamic State and '12 major counter-terrorism disruption operations'.[125] With a single exception,[126] 'the people involved in the four attacks and the people involved in the disruptions were all inspired adherents to this violent extremist interpretation of Sunni philosophy'.[127] Since these comments were made, another attack associated with Islamic State has occurred. This was a siege at a Melbourne apartment complex in June 2017, resulting in the deaths of two people (including the offender himself). In the course of this incident, the offender phoned the newsroom of a television station and said: 'This is for IS. This is for Al-Qaida'.[128]

The Australian figures are striking in light of its history of being relatively free from terrorism. Prior to 2014, it was commonly accepted that there had been no terrorist attacks on domestic soil—albeit that Australians had been targeted overseas—since the bombing of the Sydney Hilton Hotel in February 1978. A similar trend in terms of the escalation of terrorist attacks has been observed in the UK. The Home Secretary, Amber Rudd, reported that in the three months between March and June 2017 alone, there had been four terrorist attacks on UK soil, killing 36 people and injuring more than 150.[129] This may be contrasted with the absence of any completed terrorist attacks in the UK from July 2005 until the start of the Syrian civil war. In those same three months, five terrorist plots were foiled. This is in addition to the 13 terrorist plots which had been disrupted by law enforcement and intelligence agencies in the four years prior.[130]

The level of involvement of Islamic State in the aforementioned terrorist attacks and plots differs from case to case. There has, in some instances, been evidence of members of the organisation giving direct instructions to individuals or groups to carry out a terrorist attack on domestic soil. For example, the two men charged in Australia in relation to the plot to bomb an Etihad passenger airplane are alleged to have been sent military grade explosives from Islamic State.[131] Furthermore, in phone conversations with leading Islamic State recruiter, Mohammad Ali Baryalei, Australian Omarjan Azari was instructed to 'pick any random unbeliever' and, after killing them, 'put the flag of the State in the background and film it and send it off'.[132] In other instances, however, the connection has been more intangible. The hallmark of such cases has been an absence of any direct communication between members of Islamic State and those plotting the attack. Instead, the individuals and groups involved were exposed to propaganda produced by that organisation and decided independently to carry out an attack in its name. The majority of completed terrorist attacks or terrorist plots fall into this latter category. The former Independent Reviewer of Terrorism Legislation (IRTL), David Anderson, noted that '[m]ost recent UK attack plans are believed to have been inspired by Islamist extremist groups rather than directed by them, though experience shows that the dividing line is not always a clear one'.[133]

The sorts of challenges which the criminal law faces in the context of Islamic State sympathisers on domestic soil are no different to those which arise in respect of the application of the terrorism offences more generally. In fact, the existence of any connection between the individual or group involved and Islamic State is relevant—as a matter of criminal law—only as means of establishing that the acts were intended to advance a political, religious, ideological or, in the UK, racial cause. On the one hand, the offences in the UK and even more so in Australia are exceptionally broad. They capture preparatory activities which are so temporally remote from the commission of an actual terrorist act as to have been characterised by academic scholars as pre-pre-inchoate or pre-pre-crime.[134] On the other hand, however, the necessity of proving a defendant's motivation to the criminal standard of beyond a reasonable doubt operates as an impediment to securing a conviction, especially in circumstances where the authorities have intervened prior to the crystallisation of a concrete plan. It is beyond the scope of this book to reach any conclusions about the appropriateness or otherwise of these two competing aspects of the terrorism offences. It suffices to say that they raise the fundamental question of whether the criminal law is the most appropriate and effective way of responding to the foreign terrorist fighters phenomenon. Its application is inevitably limited to those circumstances in which an individual's sympathies have manifested externally (either in speech or physical conduct). Critical to responding to the foreign terrorist fighters phenomenon, however, is the development of tools for recognising the early signs of radicalisation and then preventing this from progressing.

2.4 Non-Substantive Criminal Law

This chapter has concentrated upon the extent to which the substantive criminal law, that is, the criminal offences themselves, is capable of responding to the various aspects of the threat posed by the foreign terrorist fighters phenomenon. It is also important, however, to acknowledge procedural aspects of the criminal justice system which have been modified or, in some cases, completely overhauled in an attempt to minimise this threat.

Of particular note are amendments to the bail and parole systems which make it more difficult for a person to apply for release into the community whilst awaiting trial or prior to serving their full sentence. The Criminal Justice and Courts Act 2015 (UK), for example, amended the Criminal Justice Act 2003 (UK) so that the entitlement to automatic release halfway through their sentence was removed from people convicted of serious terrorism offences.[135] In Australia, one jurisdiction—New South Wales—now requires the Parole Authority to be satisfied, prior to ordering release, that the offender will not engage in, or assist others to engage in, terrorist acts or violent extremism.[136] These new rules are not simply applicable to individuals who are currently serving a sentence of imprisonment for terrorism offences. They apply more broadly to anyone who: has previously been convicted of, or charged with, a terrorism offence; is the subject of a control order; has any associations with a terrorist organisation; has made statements or carried out activities advocating support for terrorist acts or violent extremism; or, finally, has any associations or affiliations with any person or groups advocating support for terrorist acts or violent extremism.

The significance of amendments to the bail and parole systems pales in comparison with another initiative introduced by the Australian Federal Parliament, namely, a regime of post-sentence continuing detention.[137] This is, at least in part, a reaction to several noteworthy cases in which convicted terrorists who have recently completed their sentence have travelled to the Syrian and Iraqi conflict zones. One of Australia's most prominent foreign terrorist fighters, Khaled Sharrouf, pleaded guilty in mid-2009 to possession of clocks and batteries in connection with preparation for a terrorist act.[138] After serving a period of three years and nine months in jail, he was released into the community on parole. Although his travel documentation had been cancelled, Sharrouf was nevertheless able to board a flight to Kuala Lumpur by using his brother's passport.

The relevance of the continuing detention regime is obviously not limited to the foreign terrorist fighters phenomenon. It operates generally as a way for the authorities to extend the period of time in which a convicted terrorist may be detained beyond that prescribed by the sentencing judge. A continuing detention order may be issued by the Supreme Court of a State or Territory where it is 'satisfied to a high degree of probability, on the basis of admissible evidence, that the offender poses an unacceptable risk of committing a serious [terrorism] offence if the offender is released into the community' and, furthermore, that there 'is no other less restrictive measure that would be effective in preventing the unacceptable risk'.[139] The relevance of the continuing detention regime in the foreign terrorist fighters context is that an order may be issued where there is an 'unacceptable risk' that a person will attempt to travel to the conflict zones or engage in terrorism on domestic soil, and none of the other available mechanisms, such as control orders or surveillance, would be effective in preventing that risk.

2.5 Conclusions

Whilst by no means painting a comprehensive picture, this chapter provides an insight into the various ways in which the criminal law has been utilised in the foreign terrorist fighters context as well as its limitations. In its dependence upon enforcement through the courts of the relevant jurisdiction, the criminal law is necessarily focused upon the domestic. Its operation requires not only that extraterritorial jurisdiction has been asserted, but also that the suspect returns—whether voluntarily or through coercion—to domestic soil. This throws up significant challenges so far as the 'foreign' aspect of the foreign terrorist fighters phenomenon is concerned. The efficacy of the criminal law decreases commensurate with the remoteness of an individual's behaviour from the domestic sphere. Thus, the criminal law is likely to be most effective in responding to homegrown terrorism whereupon the conduct occurs on domestic soil and the only connection with foreign terrorist organisations is ideological. On the flip side, it is likely to be particularly ineffective in addressing the actions of foreign terrorist fighters who have not returned voluntarily to their home country.

Australia has responded to these challenges by enacting additional layers of substantive criminal laws. The reality, however, is that these do not respond to the underlying problems with reliance upon the criminal justice system in the context of the foreign terrorist fighters phenomenon. It is therefore unsurprising that no returned foreign terrorist fighter, attempted foreign terrorist fighter or sympathiser on domestic soil has been prosecuted for either the advocacy offence. In December 2017, the offence of entering a declared area was used for the first time.[140]

In the opening paragraph of this chapter, reference was made to the purposes of 'a well-operating criminal justice system'. The most straightforward of these to evaluate in practice—and indeed this has been the focus of this chapter—is 'catch[ing] and punish[ing] those who commit crimes'. In other words, an assessment may be made of whether new or amended criminal offences have been relied upon as the basis for prosecutions. However, there are other more subtle ways in which criminal offences may be effective in combatting the threat of terrorism. In a 2017 report, the INSLM, James Renwick, referred to claims by the AFP, Attorney-General's Department and Australian Transaction Reports and Analysis Centre (AUSTRAC) that the declared area offence may have had a deterrent or preventive effect.[141] Such claims are, of course, difficult to test. However, the extremely cautious language used, including 'has the *potential*', '*perhaps* have also had *an* effect' and '*may* prevent', points to an absence of any concrete evidence in support of these claims.[142]

The UK Parliament has been far less reactive than its Australian counterpart in terms of enacting both substantive and procedural criminal legislation in the post-caliphate era. Its recognition of the inherent limitations of the criminal law is evident in the attention which it has given to building a civil regime—albeit also a coercive one—to combat the threat. Nevertheless, where an individual has been identified as a foreign terrorist fighter, and especially where they are alleged to have been involved with Islamic State, Al-Qaida, and their affiliates, the typical approach of the UK authorities has been to prosecute them for terrorism offences.

The large number of prosecutions in both Australia and the UK, especially of domestic sympathisers, reflects an over-concentration on the threat which the foreign terrorist fighters phenomenon poses to national security. The reality is that it is not merely national security that is placed at risk by Westerners travelling to the Syrian and Iraqi conflicts, but rather the security of the international community as a whole.[143] The fundamental problem with the default approach is that the threat posed by the foreign terrorist fighters phenomenon cannot be addressed by the use of the criminal law by individual jurisdictions. Rather, there is a need for a shift away from the criminal law towards broad-ranging counter-radicalisation strategies as playing a central—as opposed to merely supporting—role in responding to the foreign terrorist fighters phenomenon.

Notes

1   Eminent Jurists Panel on Terrorism, Counter-Terrorism and Human Rights, International Commission of Jurists, 'Assessing Damage, Urging Action' (2009) 21.
2   Department of the Parliamentary Library, Commonwealth Parliament, *Security Legislation Amendment (Terrorism) Bill 2002 [No 2] (Cth)*, No 126 of 2001–02, 30 April 2002, 19. Similarly, the Security Legislation Review Committee described the Australian and UK definitions as being 'in almost identical terms':

Security Legislation Review Committee, 'Report of the Security Legislation Review Committee' (June 2006) [6.21].

3 Terrorism Act 2006 (UK) s 1.
4 Criminal Code Act 1995 (Cth) s 80.2C.
5 See Laura K. Donohue, *Counter-Terrorist Law and Emergency Powers in the United Kingdom 1922–2000* (Dublin: Irish Academic Press, 2007).
6 Australia is the only Western democratic country without a national constitutional or statutory human rights instrument. Such instruments have been enacted at the State/Territory level in Australia by the Australian Capital Territory and Victorian Parliaments.
7 This was introduced by the Counter-Terrorism Legislation Amendment (Foreign Fighters) Act 2014 (Cth).
8 Criminal Code Act 1995 (Cth) s 119.3.
9 Criminal Code (Foreign Incursions and Recruitment—Declared Areas) Declaration 2014—Al-Raqqa Province, Syria; Criminal Code (Foreign Incursions and Recruitment—Declared Areas) Declaration 2015—Mosul District, Ninewa Province, Iraq.
10 Commonwealth, *Parliamentary Debates*, Senate, 24 September 2014, 7001-2 (George Brandis, Attorney-General).
11 Explanatory Memorandum, Counter-Terrorism Legislation Amendment (Foreign Fighters) Bill 2014 (Cth) 135.
12 Terrorism Act 2000 (UK) sch 2 s 11.
13 Terrorism Act 2006 (UK) s 8.
14 Ibid., s 5.
15 Criminal Code Act 1995 (Cth) s 15.4, applied to the terrorism offences by ss 101.1(2), 101.2(4), 101.4(4), 101.5(4), 101.6(3), 102.9, 103.3, 117.2.
16 Kent Roach, *The 9/11 Effect: Comparative Counter-Terrorism* (Cambridge: Cambridge University Press, 2011) 445.
17 [2007] EWCA Crim 234 [31].
18 Terrorism Act 2000 (UK) s 56.
19 Ibid., ss 59–61.
20 Terrorism Act 2006 (UK) s 6.
21 Ibid., s 1.
22 Ibid., s 17.
23 *Council of Europe Convention on the Prevention of Terrorism*, opened for signature 16 May 2005, CETS No 196 (entered into force 1 June 2007).
24 Joint Committee on Human Rights, *Legislative Scrutiny: (1) Serious Crime Bill, (2) Criminal Justice and Courts Bill (Second Report), and (3) Armed Forces (Service Complaints and Financial Assistance) Bill*, House of Lords Paper No 49, House of Commons Paper No 746, Session 2014–15 (2014) [1.75].
25 HM Government, *CONTEST, the United Kingdom's Strategy for Countering Terrorism: Annual Report for 2015*, Cm 9310 (2016) [2.35].
26 Australian Federal Police, 'Australian Police Obtain Arrest Warrant for Australian Involved in Syrian Conflict' (Media Release, 18 November 2015) <http://parlinfo.aph.gov.au/parlInfo/download/media/pressrel/4254094/upload_binary/4254094.pdf;fileType=application%2Fpdf#search=%22media/pressrel/4254094%22>.
27 Paul Maley, 'Arrest Warrants Await Jihadists Returning from Syrian War', *The Australian*, 12 July 2017 <www.theaustralian.com.au/news/nation/arrest-warrants-await-jihadists-returning-from-syrian-war/news-story/03a8f0790ec7cc21294d3ddd3418db96>.

28 Katharine Murphy and Gabrielle Chan, 'Turnbull Ramps Up National Security Rhetoric, Saying Australia Is "Destroying" Isis', *Guardian*, 3 March 2017 <www. theguardian.com/australia-news/2017/mar/03/turnbull-ramps-up-national-security-rhetoric-saying-australia-is-destroying-isis>.

29 Commonwealth, *Parliamentary Debates*, Senate, 25 May 2017, 188 (Duncan Lewis, Director-General of Security).

30 The remaining three are Tareq Kamleh, Neil Prakesh, and Abraham Succarieh.

31 Commonwealth, *Parliamentary Debates*, Senate, 25 May 2017, 184 (Duncan Lewis, Director-General of Security).

32 Ibid., 187.

33 Joe Kelly, 'Threat of ISIS "on Our Doorstep" with Return of Foreign Fighters, Says Julie Bishop', *The Australian*, 27 March 2017 <www.theaustralian.com. au/national-affairs/foreign-affairs/threat-of-isis-on-our-doorstep-with-return-of-foreign-fighters-says-julie-bishop/news-story/e61f083d0ef212446f291c 7797607288>.

34 James Renwick, 'Sections 119.2 and 119.3 of the Criminal Code: Declared Areas' (September 2017) 31.

35 Prakesh is currently on trial in Turkey facing charges of joining Islamic State: 'Neil Prakesh: IS Recruiter Says He Was Not "100% Responsible"', *BBC News*, 29 September 2017 <www.bbc.co.uk/news/world-australia-41437547>.

36 Commonwealth, *Parliamentary Debates*, Senate, 25 May 2017, 186 (Duncan Lewis, Director-General of Security).

37 Ibid., 183.

38 HM Government, *CONTEST, the United Kingdom's Strategy for Countering Terrorism: Annual Report for 2015*, Cm 9310 (2016) [2.35].

39 *R v Alqudsi* [2016] NSWSC 1227 [86].

40 Australian Federal Police, 'JCTT Arrests Man over Alleged Foreign Incursion Offences' (Media Release, 15 November 2016) <www.afp.gov.au/news-media/ media-releases/jctt-arrests-man-over-alleged-foreign-incursion-offences>.

41 Cf. Cameron Stewart and Paul Maley, 'Terror Trio Asks to Come Home', *The Australian*, 19 May 2015 <www.theaustralian.com.au/in-depth/terror/terror-trio-asks-to-come-home/news-story/5f3a7ce5e0bdedb57192fbe6cc94ba0d>.

42 Rory Callinan, 'Kurdish Fighter Ashley Dyball Tried to Join the Australian Army', *Sydney Morning Herald*, 11 December 2015 <www.smh.com.au/national/ kurdish-fighter-ashley-dyball-tried-to-join-the-australian-army-20151210-glkqk0.html>.

43 Ibid.

44 Mark Russell, 'Accused Melbourne Terrorist Adam Brookman in Court', *The Age*, 16 November 2015 <www.theage.com.au/victoria/accused-melbourne-terrorist-adam-brookman-in-court-20151116-gkzv1f.html>.

45 Rachel Olding, 'Syria Returnee Mehmet Biber Warns of Homegrown Attacks', *Sydney Morning Herald*, 31 January 2016 <www.smh.com.au/nsw/mehmet-biber-20150930-gjy2se.html>.

46 Commonwealth, *Parliamentary Debates*, Senate, 9 February 2016, 70 (Duncan Lewis, Director-General of Security).

47 Dan Oakes and Sam Clark, 'Sydney Man Renas Lelikan Charged over Alleged Links to Listed Terrorist Organisation PKK', *ABC News*, 20 July 2016 <www.abc.net. au/news/2016-07-20/renas-lelikan-charged-over-alleged-pkk-links/7646196>.

48 Bob de Graaff, 'How to Keep Our Youth away from IS: The Need for Narrative Analysis and Strategy' (2015) 8(5) *Journal of Strategic Security* 48, 52 (emphasis in original).

49 Jared Owens, 'Returning Islamic State Foreign Fighters Face Jail, Abbott Says', *The Australian*, 19 May 2015 <www.theaustralian.com.au/in-depth/terror/returning-islamic-state-foreign-fighters-face-jail-abbott-says/news-story/0287c93eb9f da0c2f3d55b5c8a456ea4>.

50 Georgina Mitchell, 'Senior Labor Figure Matthew Gardiner Leaves Australia to Fight Against Islamic State: Report', *Sydney Morning Herald*, 25 January 2015 <www.smh.com.au/national/senior-labor-figure-matthew-gardiner-leaves-australia-to-fight-against-islamic-state-report-20150125-12xu6g.html>.

51 Tim Legrand, 'We Should Be Using Returning Foreign Fighters Against Islamic State', *The Drum*, 20 May 2015 <www.abc.net.au/news/2015-05-20/legrand-foreign-fighters-can-help-us-battle-islamic-state/6484590>.

52 Matthew Knott, 'No Charge for Suspected Foreign Fighters Matthew Gardiner and George Khamis', *Sydney Morning Herald*, 20 May 2015 <www.smh.com.au/federal-politics/political-news/no-charges-for-suspected-foreign-fighters-matthew-gardiner-and-george-khamis-20150520-gh61nn.html>.

53 'Iraq Crisis: Scott Morrison Defends Plan to Supply Arms and Ammunition to Kurdish Peshmerga; US Strikes near Mosul Dam; UN to Send Investigators', *ABC News*, 2 September 2014 <www.abc.net.au/news/2014-09-01/immigration-minister-scott-morrison-denies-weapons-claims/5711608>.

54 Richard Norton-Taylor, 'Terror Trial Collapses After Fears of Deep Embarrassment to Security Services', *Guardian*, 1 June 2015 <www.theguardian.com/uk-news/2015/jun/01/trial-swedish-man-accused-terrorism-offences-collapse-bherlin-gildo>.

55 Ibid.

56 Matthew Knott, 'No Charge for Suspected Foreign Fighters Matthew Gardiner and George Khamis', *Sydney Morning Herald*, 20 May 2015 <www.smh.com.au/federal-politics/political-news/no-charges-for-suspected-foreign-fighters-matthew-gardiner-and-george-khamis-20150520-gh61nn.html>.

57 ABC Radio National, 'Calls for Terror Laws to Distinguish Between Foreign Fighters Supporting and Opposing Islamic State', *RN Breakfast*, 31 May 2016 (Fran Kelly) <www.abc.net.au/radionational/programs/breakfast/calls-for-terror-laws-to-be-amended-to-distinguish/7462256>.

58 Ibid.

59 Cf. the example of Australians fighting in South Sudan: Colin Cosier, 'Aussies in South Sudan Conflict Put Australian Law to the Test', *Sydney Morning Herald*, 17 July 2016 <www.smh.com.au/world/do-these-six-australians-have-a-case-to-answer-20160622-gpozja.html>.

60 Bret Walker, 'Annual Report' (28 March 2014) 31.

61 Ibid., 33–4.

62 Criminal Code Act 1995 (Cth) s 119.2.

63 Bret Walker, 'Annual Report' (28 March 2014) 31.

64 Foreign Evidence Act 1994 (Cth) s 27C.

65 HM Government, *CONTEST, the United Kingdom's Strategy for Countering Terrorism: Annual Report for 2015*, Cm 9310 (2016) [2.35].

66 Robert Mendick and Robert Verkaik, 'Only One in Eight Jihadists Returning to UK Is Caught and Convicted', *The Telegraph*, 21 May 2016 <www.telegraph.co.uk/news/2016/05/21/only-one-in-eight-jihadists-returning-to-uk-is-caught-and-convic>.

67 United Kingdom, *Parliamentary Debates*, House of Lords, 28 April 2016, HL8065 (Lord Keen of Elie).

68 'Who Are Britain's Jihadists?', *BBC News*, 5 July 2017 <www.bbc.co.uk/news/uk-32026985>.
69 Steve Swann, 'UK Terror Convictions Rising, BBC Jihadists Database Shows', *BBC News*, 6 July 2017 <www.bbc.co.uk/news/uk-40483171>.
70 Crown Prosecution Service, *Briton Jailed for Terrorist Activity in Syria* (6 February 2015) <www.cps.gov.uk/news/latest_news/briton_jailed_for_terrorist_activity_in_syria/>.
71 'R v Imran Khawaja, Tahir Bhatti, Asim Ali, Sentencing Remarks of Mr Justice Jeremy Baker' (Woolwich Crown Court, 6 February 2015) [24] <www.judiciary.gov.uk/wp-content/uploads/2015/02/khawaja-sentencing-remarks1.pdf>.
72 'Britons Fighting in Iraq and Syria May Face Treason Charges If They Return', *Guardian*, 17 October 2014 <www.theguardian.com/world/2014/oct/17/isis-syria-iraq-britons-treason-charges-philip-hammond>.
73 Liam Byrne, 'Time to Charge Britain's ISIS Fighters with Genocide', *The Times*, 20 September 2017 <www.thetimes.co.uk/article/time-to-charge-britains-isis-fighters-with-genocide-fwlhzvxnw>.
74 Press Association, 'London Jihadi Found Guilty of Possessing Terror Training Videos', *Guardian*, 15 December 2015 <www.theguardian.com/uk-news/2015/dec/15/london-jihadi-guilty-terror-training-videos-mustafa-abdullah>.
75 Ben Mitchell and Caroline Mortimer, 'Mohammed Uddin: British Man Jailed After Going to Syria to Join ISIS', *The Independent*, 10 February 2016 <www.independent.co.uk/news/uk/crime/isis-syria-british-man-mohammed-uddin-a6865291.html>.
76 Steven Morris, 'British Woman Who Joined Isis Is Jailed for Six Years', *Guardian*, 1 February 2016 <www.theguardian.com/uk-news/2016/feb/01/british-woman-tareena-shakil-convicted-being-isis-member-jailed-xx-years>.
77 Terrorism Act 2006 (UK) s 1.
78 Ibid., s 11.
79 Edwin Bakker and Roel de Bont, 'Belgian and Dutch Jihadist Foreign Fighters (2012–2015): Characteristics, Motivations, and Roles in the War in Syria and Iraq' (2016) 27 *Small Wars & Insurgencies* 837, 848.
80 Steven Morris, 'British Woman Who Joined Isis Is jailed for Six Years', *Guardian*, 1 February 2016 <www.theguardian.com/uk-news/2016/feb/01/british-woman-tareena-shakil-convicted-being-isis-member-jailed-xx-years>.
81 'R v Imran Khawaja, Tahir Bhatti, Asim Ali, Sentencing Remarks of Mr Justice Jeremy Baker' (Woolwich Crown Court, 6 February 2015) [24] <www.judiciary.gov.uk/wp-content/uploads/2015/02/khawaja-sentencing-remarks1.pdf>.
82 Terrorism Act 2006 (UK) s 8.
83 Dominic Casciani, 'British Brothers Jailed for Training at Syria Terror Camp', *BBC News*, 26 November 2014 <www.bbc.co.uk/news/uk-30213771>.
84 Joseph Smith, 'Bristol Man Who Fought Against ISIS Faces Terror Charge Trial—Because of Book', *Bristol Post*, 18 July 2017 <www.bristolpost.co.uk/news/bristol-news/bristol-man-who-fought-against-209179>.
85 Owen Bowcott, 'British Teenage Girl Charged with Trying to Join Kurdish Forces Fighting ISIS', *Guardian*, 14 March 2015 <www.theguardian.com/world/2015/mar/13/british-teenage-girl-charged-kurdish-forces-fighting-isis>.
86 Ryan Gallagher, 'To Syria and Back', *The Intercept*, 10 July 2017 <https://theintercept.com/2017/07/10/josh-walker-isis-uk-terrorism-charge-ypg-syria/>.
87 Lizzie Dearden, 'Joshua Walker: Student Who Fought Against ISIS in Syria Cleared of Terror Charges over Book He Owned', *Guardian*, 26 October 2017

<www.independent.co.uk/news/uk/crime/joshua-walker-verdict-anarchists-cookbook-isis-syria-trial-uk-fighter-ypg-role-play-game-a8022126.html>.

88 United Kingdom, *Parliamentary Debates*, House of Commons, 19 April 2016, vol. 608, col. 893 (Robert Jenrick).

89 *R v Sarwar* [2015] EWCA Crim 1886.

90 Ibid., [41]. This may be contrasted with the approach taken by the prosecution of Bherlin Gildo.

91 Ibid.

92 The information in this paragraph is taken from *R v Mohamed* [2016] VSC 581. Indeed, the relationship between the two men was the factual basis of one of the counts against Alqudsi.

93 Ibid., [26].

94 Ibid., [29].

95 Stephanie Gardiner, 'Fatima Elomar Pleads Guilty to Helping Husband's Islamic State Fight in Syria', *Sydney Morning Herald*, 16 November 2015 <www.smh.com.au/nsw/fatima-elomar-pleads-guilty-to-helping-husbands-islamic-state-fight-in-syria-20151116-gkzv6v.html>.

96 Michael Safi, 'Foreign Fighter Case Dropped against Man Accused of Trying to Fight with Kurdish Rebels', *Guardian*, 9 February 2016 <www.theguardian.com/australia-news/2016/feb/09/foreign-fighter-case-dropped-against-man-accused-of-trying-to-fight-with-kurdish-rebels>.

97 Ibid.

98 Ibid.

99 'Two Britons Freed in Iraq on Way Home from Fighting ISIS', *Guardian*, 24 April 2016 <www.theguardian.com/world/2016/apr/24/two-britons-freed-in-iraq-after-arrest-on-way-home-from-fighting-isis>.

100 Terrorism Act 2006 (UK) s 5.

101 Dominic Casciani, 'Low IQ Teen Convicted for Syria Plan', *BBC News*, 13 November 2015 <www.bbc.com/news/uk-34814735>.

102 Dominic Casciani, 'Walsall to Syria: Fighters, Travellers and Victims?', *BBC News*, 24 February 2016 <www.bbc.com/news/uk-35631699>. Other examples include Mudassir Hussain, Humza Ali, and Jamila Henry.

103 David Barrett, 'Bungling Jihadi Complained He Was Forced to "Walk Across Europe" to Reach ISIL', *The Telegraph*, 27 May 2015 <www.telegraph.co.uk/news/uknews/terrorism-in-the-uk/11633434/Bungling-jihadi-complained-he-was-forced-to-walk-across-Europe-to-reach-Isil.html>.

104 For example, David Souaan and Jamshed Javeed.

105 For example, Ghulam Hussain.

106 For example, Patrick Kabele.

107 For example, Shivan Zangana, Aras Hamid, Mohammed Mayow, Mohanned Jasim, Gabriel Rasmus, Anas Abdalla and Mahamuud Diini.

108 Dan Oakes and Sam Clark, 'Islamic Preacher Musa Cerantonio Among Five Arrested over Alleged Plan to Join Islamic State', *ABC News*, 11 May 2016 <www.abc.net.au/news/2016-05-11/preacher-among-five-arrested-over-alleged-plan-to-join-is/7403344>.

109 David Gayle and Jamie Grierson, 'London Attack: Khuram Butt's Family Stopped Him Going to Syria, Says Cousin', *Guardian*, 9 June 2017 <www.theguardian.com/uk-news/2017/jun/08/london-attack-wounded-policeman-tells-families-i-did-everything-i-could>.

110 'Trainee Teacher Guilty of Not Revealing Husband's IS Plans', *BBC News*, 24 February 2016 <www.bbc.com/news/uk-35653366>.

111 'Syria Conflict: Portsmouth Brothers Jailed for Terrorism Offences', *BBC News*, 18 November 2015 <www.bbc.co.uk/news/uk-england-hampshire-34847044>.

112 Commonwealth, *Parliamentary Debates*, Senate, 25 May 2017, 183–4 (Duncan Lewis, Director-General of Security).

113 '23,000 People Have Been "Subjects of Interest" as Scale of Terror Threat Emerges After Manchester Attack', *The Telegraph*, 27 May 2017 <www.telegraph.co.uk/news/2017/05/27/23000-people-have-subjects-interest-scale-terror-threat-emerges/>.

114 Home Office, 'Operation of Police Powers Under the Terrorism Act 2000 and Subsequent Legislation: Arrests, Outcomes, and Stop and Search, Great Britain, Quarterly Update to June 2017' (Statistical Bulletin 14/17, September 2017) 14. 'International' refers to 'activity by an individual or group of individuals (regardless of nationality) linked to or motivated by any terrorist group that is based outside the UK which operate in and from third countries': at 14, n 1.

115 Press Association, 'Woman Jailed for Twitter Terrorism', *Guardian*, 11 June 2015 <www.theguardian.com/uk-news/2015/jun/11/alaa-esayed-jail-twitter-terrorism-london>.

116 Terrorism Act 2006 (UK) s 1.

117 Ibid., s 2.

118 Ibid., s 12(1).

119 *R v Kahar* [2016] EWCA Crim 568.

120 Ibid.

121 See Sean Gates and Sukanya Podder, 'Social Media, Recruitment, Allegiance and the Islamic State' (2015) 9(4) *Perspectives on Terrorism* 107; Jytte Klausen, 'Tweeting the *Jihad*: Social Media Networks of Western Foreign Fighters in Syria and Iraq' (2015) 38 *Studies in Conflict and Terrorism* 1.

122 '"Cufflink" Terrorist Samata Ullah Admits IS Charges', *BBC News*, 20 March 2017 <www.bbc.com/news/uk-wales-south-east-wales-39326533>.

123 In December 2016, a South Australian man was charged with advocating terrorism in relation to videos posted on social media which provided explicit verbal instructions as well as physical demonstrations with weapons as to how to kill Jewish people.

124 *R v El Sabsabi* [2016] VSC 740 [13]–[18].

125 Commonwealth, *Parliamentary Debates*, Senate, 25 May 2017, 183 (Duncan Lewis, Director-General of Security).

126 See n 123.

127 Commonwealth, *Parliamentary Debates*, Senate, 28 February 2017, 116 (Duncan Lewis, Director-General of Security).

128 'Brighton Siege: Melbourne Police Launch Terror Probe, Investigate If Escort Was Used to Lure Officers', *ABC News*, 6 July 2017 <www.abc.net.au/news/2017-06-06/islamic-state-claims-responsibility-for-brighton-siege/8591540>.

129 United Kingdom, *Parliamentary Debates*, House of Commons, 22 June 2017, vol. 626, col. 195 (Amber Rudd, Home Secretary).

130 National Counter-Terrorism Security Office, 'Action Counters Terrorism' (7 March 2017) <www.gov.uk/government/news/action-counters-terrorism>.

131 Ava Benny-Morrison and Rachel Olding, 'Islamic State Sent "Military-Grade Explosive" to Australia Undetected as Part of Alleged Terror Plot', *Sydney*

Morning Herald, 5 August 2017 <www.smh.com.au/nsw/islamic-state-sent-militarygrade-explosive-australia-undetected-20170804-gxpqin.html>.

132 Louise Hall, '"Just Pick Any Random Unbeliever": Court Hears Transcript of Alleged Omarjan Azari Phone Call', *Sydney Morning Herald*, 24 February 2015 <www.smh.com.au/nsw/just-pick-any-random-unbeliever-court-hears-transcript-of-alleged-omarjan-azari-phone-call-20150224-13n9av.html>.

133 David Anderson, 'The Terrorism Acts in 2015' (December 2016) 11.

134 See Jude McCulloch, 'Human Rights and Terror Laws' (2015) 128 *Precedent* 26, 28.

135 Criminal Justice and Courts Act 2015 (UK) sch 1.

136 These changes were introduced in the Terrorism Legislation Amendment (Police Powers and Parole) Act 2017 (NSW).

137 Criminal Code (High Risk Terrorist Offenders) Act 2016 (Cth), inserting div 105A into the Criminal Code Act 1995 (Cth).

138 *R v Sharrouf* [2009] NSWSC 1002 [5].

139 Criminal Code Act 1995 (Cth) s 105A.7(1).

140 James Renwick, 'Sections 119.2 and 119.3 of the Criminal Code: Declared Areas' (September 2017) 31. The AFP also gave evidence to the INSLM that 'a number' of outstanding arrest warrants include the declared area offence, such as those in relation to Tareq Kamleh and Neil Prakesh. On 19 December 2017, a 25 year old Australian man was charged under section 119.2 of the Criminal Code. He is the first Australian to be charged with the declared area offence, but the case has not yet gone to trial. See AFP, 'Sydney Man Charged over Alleged Foreign Fighter Links' <www.afp.gov.au/news-media/media-releases/sydney-man-charged-over-alleged-foreign-fighter-links>.

141 Ibid., 30.

142 Ibid., citing submissions and oral evidence by the AFP, Attorney-General's Department and AUSTRAC.

143 See Chapter 4 at 85–6.

3 Hybrid Sanctions

3.1 Introduction

As is discussed in Chapter 2, Australia and the UK rely heavily upon the criminal justice system in responding to the threat posed by terrorism. However, the inability of this system to adequately address all facets of the threat means that both jurisdictions have also created alternative administrative and civil regimes to counter terrorism.[1] The purpose of such regimes—as indeed with most facets of anti-terrorism legislation—is preventive, that is, to stop terrorism before it occurs. The use of preventive non-criminal regimes is, of course, not unique to the counter-terrorism context. Andrew Ashworth and Lucia Zedner note that 'recourse to civil and hybrid-criminal preventive measures has been an important feature of lawmaking since the 1990s'.[2] UK examples include Anti-Social Behaviour Orders and non-molestation orders. Australian jurisdictions have similarly established civil and administrative regimes to preventively detain high-risk sex offenders and people with mental illnesses.[3] The particular regimes established since September 11 to prevent terrorism are, however, distinct in their impact on the rights of those subject to them. Ashworth and Zedner emphasise that 'it is in respect of the potentially catastrophic risks posed by terrorism that the most intrusive and far-reaching measures, with the greatest impact upon individual liberty, have been introduced'.[4] They term this new form of measure 'hybrid civil-criminal'.[5]

Such measures are similar to the earlier civil and administrative regimes in that they require only the civil standard of proof to be met. However, they also engage the criminal law by imposing a criminal penalty for breach. This type of measure was first established in the UK in March 2005, under the now repealed Prevention of Terrorism Act (PTA).[6] This Act empowered the Home Secretary to issue a control order imposing any conditions they considered to be 'necessary for purposes connected with preventing or restricting involvement by that individual in terrorism-related activity'.[7] Before making an order, two conditions had to be satisfied: first, that there were reasonable grounds for suspecting that the individual was involved in terrorism-related activity; and second, that making the control order was necessary 'for purposes connected with protecting members of the public from a risk of terrorism'.[8] Breach of any of the conditions of the control order was a criminal offence, punishable by a maximum penalty of five years imprisonment.[9] In December 2005, in response to the terrorist attacks in London five months earlier, the Australian Federal Parliament enacted Division 104 of the Criminal Code. This had the effect of transplanting the substance of the UK's control order regime to Australia.[10] Whilst Australia has retained its control order regime, the UK Parliament replaced its original regime with a system of Terrorism Prevention and Investigation Measures (TPIMs) in 2011.[11]

Control orders and TPIMs were introduced in Australia and the UK well in advance of the Syrian and Iraqi conflicts. They were thus not specifically designed to address the threat posed by foreign terrorist fighters. Both regimes have, however, been adapted in response to that phenomenon. This chapter outlines the original regimes and charts the amendments which have been introduced in Australia and the UK since 2014, before evaluating their effectiveness as a response to the foreign terrorist fighters phenomenon.

The Australian control order regime and the UK's system of TPIMs share a number of core features. Both regimes include a list of 12 similar—albeit not identical—obligations, prohibitions, and restrictions that may be imposed on a person subject to an order.[12] The length of an order is also similar in both jurisdictions, with a control order or TPIM applying for up to one year.[13] In the UK, a TPIM can be extended once, for an additional 12 months.[14] No such extension is possible under Division 104 in Australia; however, there is also nothing to stop successive control orders from being made against the same individual.[15] Breach of a control order[16] or a TPIM[17] is a criminal offence, punishable by a maximum sentence of five years imprisonment.

One of the primary differences between the current Australian and UK regimes concerns the issuing authority. In Australia, a senior member of the Australian Federal Police (AFP) must seek the consent of the Attorney-General before applying to the court for an interim control order.[18] The interim control order must specify: the grounds on which the control order is made; the list of obligations, prohibitions, and restrictions to be imposed; and the date on which the court will hold a hearing to determine whether to confirm the control order.[19] The confirmation hearing must be held 'as soon as practicable, but at least 72 hours, after the order is made', with the issuing court taking into account the time needed by the parties to prepare.[20] If the senior AFP member does not elect to confirm the interim control order, then it ceases to have effect.[21] In contrast, in the UK, TPIMs are issued by the Home Secretary. This can only be done, however, with the prior consent of the court or where the urgency of the case justifies the issuing of a TPIM without such consent.[22]

The system of TPIMs also deviates from the Australian control order regime—as introduced in 2005—in that TPIM proceedings are subject to special rules of the court. These rules prevent the disclosure of certain material to the subject of the TPIM and their legal representative,[23] as well as excluding them from hearings involving that material.[24] To mitigate the effects of these special rules, the court can appoint a special advocate, that is, 'a person to represent the interests of a party in any TPIM proceedings or appeal proceedings from which the party (and any legal representative of the party) is excluded'.[25]

In its original form, there was no provision under the Australian control order regime for proceedings to be held either in closed court or in the absence of the controlee. As such, special advocates were not considered necessary. However, Division 104 did allow for certain documents to be withheld where the disclosure of their contents may 'prejudice national security'.[26] These documents included: the summary of grounds upon which the AFP member sought the Attorney-General's consent;[27] the summary of grounds on which an interim control order was made;[28] material that must be served on a person when a control order was confirmed, including any 'written details required to enable the person to understand and respond to the substance of the facts, matters, and circumstances which will form the basis of the confirmation of the order';[29] and, information relating to the variation of a confirmed control order.[30] This arrangement has faced criticism from two different angles. On the one hand, the potential for the aforementioned documents to be withheld represented a substantial practical impediment to anyone trying to challenge an interim or confirmed control order. On the other hand, the Australian Government argued that because 'the ordinary rules of evidence apply in relation to control order proceedings before issuing courts',[31] 'an issuing court cannot presently make a control order based on material which a controlee has not seen'.[32] This was queried by the former Independent National Security Legislation Monitor (INSLM), Roger Gyles. He noted: 'The proposition that div 104 does not permit the applicant for a control order to rely on information withheld or to be withheld from the controlee is debatable'.[33] Nevertheless, in response to the foreign terrorist fighters phenomenon, the Australian Federal Parliament enacted legislation which clarified the situation. The introduction of closed material proceedings like those in the UK in control order proceedings and the establishment of a system of special advocates is discussed in the next section of this chapter, alongside other amendments to Division 104.

3.2 Changes to the Australian Control Order Regime

Recent amendments made to the control order regime were predicated on the Australian Government's assertion that 'Australia faces a serious and ongoing terrorist threat',[34] both from the 'escalating terrorist situation in Iraq and Syria'[35] and the 'risk posed by returning foreign fighters'.[36] New legislation was needed, the Explanatory Memorandum to the Foreign Fighters Bill explained, because '[e]xisting legislation does not adequately address the domestic security threats posed by the return of Australians who have participated in foreign conflicts or undertaken training with extremist groups overseas'.[37] Despite these claims, only four control orders have been issued since the start of the Syrian and Iraqi conflicts. Before looking at whether these orders relied upon the recent amendments to the control order regime—thus revealing their effectiveness—this chapter will provide a brief description of the factual background to each.

Two interim control orders were issued against unnamed individuals on 17 December 2014. Shortly thereafter, one of those individuals was arrested during terrorism raids in western Sydney.[38] At trial, the unnamed man, referred to as 'MO', pleaded guilty to the offence of breaching an interim control order and was sentenced to two years imprisonment. MO admitted that he had violated the conditions of the order by 'using a public telephone on two occasions, one very shortly after the other, and by using a mobile telephone on another occasion'.[39] He was released on parole on 22 June 2016, but was returned to custody on another matter.[40] Neither the interim control order against MO, nor that against the other unnamed individual, was confirmed by the court.[41]

Two confirmed control orders have also been issued, one against Ahmad Saiyer Naizmand[42] and the other against Harun Causevic.[43] An interim control order was issued against Naizmand on 5 March 2015. It was confirmed, with minor amendments to five of the conditions, in November that year.[44] In 2013, prior to the issuing of the control order, Naizmand's passport had been cancelled because of security concerns and, in 2014, he had been convicted of using his brother's passport in an attempt to leave Australia to join Islamic State.[45] The confirmed control order was due to lapse on 6 March 2016, however, just a week beforehand, Naizmand was arrested for breaching the prohibition on accessing terrorist materials.[46] According to the Supreme Court of New South Wales, 'the applicant accessed electronic media depicting or describing propaganda or promotional material for a terrorist organisation, or of activities associated with Islamic State, or explosives, suicide attacks, bombings or terrorist attacks'.[47] Naizmand was denied bail at a hearing in June 2016[48] and, following a guilty plea at trial, he was sentenced to four years imprisonment.[49]

An interim control order was issued against Harun Causevic on 10 September 2015.[50] In the previous five months, Causevic had been placed in preventative detention[51] as well as being charged with terrorism.[52] Those charges related to a foiled plot to kill a policeman during the 2015 Anzac Day commemorations.[53] The charges against Causevic were formally withdrawn due to a lack of evidence; however, his co-conspirator, Sevdet Besim, was convicted, as well as another teenager in the UK.[54] Causevic's interim control order was confirmed on 8 July 2016,[55] albeit with a number of the controls varied.[56] As no further orders were sought by the AFP, the order lapsed on 11 September 2016. At the time of writing, no interim or confirmed control orders are in force in Australia.

The control orders issued against the two unnamed individuals, Naizmand and Causevic offer only limited material on which to base an evaluation of the effectiveness of the recent amendments to the control order regime. Those amendments primarily concern the grounds and terms on which a control order may be sought by the AFP and issued by the court, the age of controlees, and as already mentioned above, the introduction of closed material proceedings and special advocates in control order hearings. Tentative conclusions can, however, be drawn based on an assessment of the extent to which the changes have been relied upon in these four cases.

The first set of changes to Division 104 in response to the foreign terrorist fighters phenomenon relates to the process of seeking and issuing a control order. The Foreign Fighters Act lowered the subjective threshold that an AFP member has to meet before seeking the Attorney-General's consent from 'considers on reasonable grounds' to reasonable suspicion.[57] This amendment was made following 'law enforcement advice that the current threshold for seeking consent to apply for an interim control order is too high'.[58] It 'means that an AFP applicant can request the Attorney-General's consent for a control order based on a lower degree of certainty as to whether a control order would "substantially assist in preventing a terrorist act"'.[59]

The grounds to which reasonable suspicion attaches were also expanded in response to the foreign fighters phenomenon. Prior to 2014, a senior AFP member could only seek the Attorney-General's consent to apply to the court for an interim control order on the basis either that 'the order . . . would substantially assist in preventing a terrorist act' or 'the person has provided training to, or received training from, a listed terrorist organisation'.[60] Amendments made in 2014 and 2016 expanded these grounds to include reasonable suspicion that: the person has engaged in a hostile activity in a foreign country; they have been convicted in Australia or in a foreign country of a terrorism offence; they have provided support for, or otherwise facilitated, the engagement in a hostile activity in a foreign country; or, the control order would prevent the provision of support for, or the facilitation of, a terrorist act.[61] Similar changes were made to the grounds of which the issuing court has to be satisfied on the balance of probabilities before issuing a control order.[62]

In addition, in its original form, the control order regime required the issuing court to be 'satisfied on the balance of probabilities' that the terms of the order were 'reasonably necessary, and reasonably appropriate and adapted, for the purpose of protecting the public from a terrorist act'. Again in 2014, Division 104 was amended such that the court need only be satisfied that the order is reasonably necessary, and reasonably appropriate and adapted, for the purpose of *any* of the objects of the Division. Prior to the start of the Syrian and Iraqi conflicts, the sole object was 'to allow obligations, prohibitions and restrictions to be imposed on a person by a control order for the purpose of protecting the public from a terrorist act'.[63] Two further objects have since been included: preventing the provision of support for, or the facilitation of, a terrorist act; and, preventing the provision of support for, or the facilitation of, the engagement in a hostile activity in a foreign country.

Those amendments were necessary, according to the Minister for Justice, Michael Keenan, to enable 'the Australian Federal Police to seek control orders in relation to individuals of security concern not currently captured by that regime'.[64] They included people who 'enable' and 'recruit', but 'may not directly participate in terrorist acts',[65] as well as those who 'have provided support or facilitated Australians either to engage in terrorism offences in Australia or to travel to conflict zones and return to Australia with capabilities acquired from fighting or training with proscribed terrorist groups'.[66] The amendments reflect the Australian Security Intelligence Organisation's (ASIO) concern that along with the estimated 100 Australians thought to be actively fighting in the Syrian and Iraqi conflicts, approximately 200 others are being investigated for providing support to individuals and organisations involved in those conflicts.[67]

Despite the Australian Government's assertions that it was necessary to extend the grounds on which a control order could be sought and issued, the use of such orders in the three years since the declaration of a caliphate by Islamic State tells a very different story. Of the four control orders issued during that period, at least three were issued on the original ground of preventing a terrorist act.[68] In issuing the interim control order against Naizmand, the Federal Circuit Court of Australia confirmed that it was 'satisfied on the balance of probabilities that making the order would substantially assist in preventing a terrorist act'.[69] The summary of the grounds on which the interim control order against Causevic was made referred to the need to 'protect the public and substantially assist in preventing a terrorist act'.[70] In the confirmation hearing, Justice Hartnett stated that he was 'satisfied on the balance of probabilities that confirming the Interim Control Order [against Causevic] would substantially assist in preventing a terrorist act'.[71] The control orders against Naizmand and Causevic were each issued on the basis that the court was satisfied on the balance of probabilities that each of the obligations, prohibitions, and restrictions was reasonably necessary, and reasonably appropriate and adapted, for the purpose of protecting the public from a terrorist act.[72]

Whilst there is no published information about the terms of the interim control orders issued against the two unnamed people, it can be inferred from the sentencing remarks in respect of MO that the order against him was likely issued for the purpose of protecting 'members of the public from terrorist acts'.[73] The current INSLM, James Renwick, has noted that the control order against the other unnamed individual was issued on the same grounds.[74] None of the four control orders issued since the start of the Syrian and Iraqi conflicts therefore relied on the additional grounds introduced in response to the foreign terrorist fighters phenomenon.

In spite of the lack of reliance upon these grounds, Renwick nevertheless asserts that they 'relate to real and continuing threats'.[75] To support this claim, he highlights the hypothetical possibility of 'circumstances in which intelligence from abroad supports preventative action, such as a control order, against a foreign fighter who has returned to Australia but this intelligence is not sufficient to mount a prosecution'.[76] However, here we run into the same problem identified in Chapter 2 regarding the prosecution of returned foreign terrorist fighters. Control orders can only be imposed in these circumstances if that individual decides to return, or is returned against their will, to Australia.[77] In circumstances in which they are already in Australia, past use of the control order regime indicates that it was already capable—in its pre-amendment form—of applying.

The second set of amendments to the control order regime relate to the age of controlees. In 2016, the minimum age at which a person could be subject to a control order was lowered from 16 to 14 years of age.[78] This change was accompanied by the introduction of new safeguards which apply to control orders against minors. They include a requirement that in determining whether the control order is 'reasonably necessary, and reasonably appropriate and adapted', the issuing court must, as a primary consideration, take into account the 'best interests of the person'.[79] The safeguards also set a three month limit on the duration of a confirmed control order against a minor.[80] These changes were introduced in response to a perceived increase in terrorism-related activities by younger teenagers, both in Australia and as part of the wider foreign terrorist fighters phenomenon.[81] The Explanatory Memorandum to the Counter-Terrorism Amendment Bill explained that 'the age limit of 16 years is no longer sufficient if control orders are to be effective in preventing terrorist activity'.[82] The

Attorney-General, George Brandis, further justified lowering the age on the basis that:

> Recent counter terrorism operations have unfortunately shown that people as young as 14 years of age can pose a significant risk to national security through their involvement in planning and supporting terrorist acts. In this context, it is important that our law enforcement and national security agencies are well equipped to respond to, and prevent, terrorist acts. This is the case even where the threats are posed by people under the age of 18 years.[83]

This amendment only came into effect in 2016, that is, after the control orders against the two unnamed people, Naizmand and Causevic had already been issued. Despite the Australian Government's concerns about the risk posed by children participating in terrorist activity, no control orders have been issued against children—or, in fact, against anyone—since the changes were introduced. This is particularly striking given that Naizmand's interim control order prohibited him from associating with a 12-year-old boy who was considered by the AFP to be a security concern. That individual turned 14 shortly before the amendments were enacted.[84] In his recent review of control orders, the INSLM, James Renwick, stated that he had been 'persuaded by the evidence and information' that he 'received for this review that persons aged 14 to 17 years of age contribute to the threat picture' and that 'applying the control order regime to these persons remains a necessary and proportionate response to the terrorist threat'.[85]

As is noted in Chapter 2, lack of use does not necessarily indicate lack of effectiveness. Even in the absence of any control orders issued against 14- and 15-year-olds, it is worthwhile making some general remarks about the trend in government policy towards extending coercive legislative measures to younger individuals. Citizenship revocation—as is discussed in Chapter 4—already applies to children as young as 14.[86] So far as the criminal law is concerned, this trend is evidenced in the recent proposal to permit 10-year-olds to be detained pre-charge for up to 14 days.[87] These proposals are predicated on the idea that children pose a significant threat of terrorism. However, the emphasis on young people is misguided. Of the recent terrorist attacks in Australia which were inspired by Islamic extremism, only one was perpetrated by a minor. Farhad Jabar was 15 when he killed Curtis Cheng. The involvement of older individuals is also seen in recent foiled plots, such as the plot to place a bomb on an Etihad Airlines plane. In that case, the suspects were aged 32 and 49 at the time they were charged with doing acts in preparation or planning for a terrorist act.[88]

There is, however, a more fundamental objection to the lowering of the age on control orders. The criminal law has long recognised its limitations in dealing with minors who are not aware of the difference between right and wrong. These hybrid civil-criminal measures are no different. Whilst control orders may not deprive those subject to them of their liberty in the same sense as a prison sentence, they do include serious restrictions on the liberties of the subject and attract criminal sanctions on breach. It may even be possible for someone serving a sentence for breach of a control order to be subject to continuing detention, under the new post-sentence detention regime outlined in Chapter 2.[89] The INSLM, James Renwick, noted that the 'significant criminal penalties for breaching a control order'[90] cast doubt on the claim that such orders offer an alternative to the formal criminal justice system for diverting young people away from violent extremism. Renwick further noted that 'the control order regime should not be used solely as a form of behaviour management or supervision, as to do so would be to take the regime outside its stated objectives'.[91] Alternative programmes, such as community-run early intervention schemes, are likely to be both more appropriate and more effective in dealing with vulnerable teenagers than any coercive body of legislation.

The third set of amendments to the control order regime involved the introduction of closed material proceedings and the concomitant establishment of a special advocates scheme. These measures, like the control order regime itself, have been transplanted in large part from the UK. Provisions relating to 'special court orders' in control order proceedings were inserted into the National Security Information (Criminal and Civil Proceedings) Act (NSIA) in 2016. These enable the Attorney-General or their legal representative to request that the court make a non-disclosure order relating to information, whether in documentary or any other form, or witness evidence.[92] The effect of such an order is to require the court to consider the relevant material in a closed hearing from which the controlee and their legal representative are excluded.[93] Before it issues a non-disclosure order, the court must be 'satisfied that the relevant person has been given sufficient information about the allegations on which the control order request was based to enable effective instructions to be given in relation to those allegations'.[94] This ostensibly ensures a minimum standard of disclosure to the controlee.

To mitigate the potentially adverse effects of closed material proceedings, a system of special advocates was also introduced. This implemented recommendations of the former INSLM, Roger Gyles,[95] and the Council of Australian Governments (COAG) Review of Counter-Terrorism Legislation.[96] The court may appoint a special advocate in control order proceedings where the controlee and their legal representative are excluded from the hearing.[97] The special advocate is neither a party to the proceeding[98] nor the legal representative of the controlee.[99] However, it is the function of the special advocate to represent the interests of the controlee by making written and oral submissions to the court, adducing evidence and cross-examining witnesses.[100] The special advocate is granted access to all of the material subject to a non-disclosure order[101] but, because of this, they are prohibited from communicating with the controlee and their legal representative after the information has been disclosed.[102] The court may also prohibit or restrict communication between the special advocate on the one hand and the controlee and their legal representative on the other, prior to the disclosure of information if it is 'in the interest of national security' to do so.[103] The Explanatory Memorandum to the Counter-Terrorism Amendment Bill explained the rationale for the introduction of a system of special advocates:

> In light of the current threat environment, it is increasingly likely that law enforcement will need to rely on evidence that is extremely sensitive in nature, such that disclosure, even to a security-cleared lawyer, could compromise the safety of human sources and the integrity of ongoing police investigations. In the absence of the amendments contained in Part 1 of Schedule 15 there is a substantial risk that the inability to rely on, and protect, sensitive information may result in a control order being unable to be obtained against an individual who poses a risk to the safety of the community.[104]

These amendments were enacted in November 2016, long after the four control orders discussed in this chapter had lapsed. They have, as a result, not yet been used. This seems counter-intuitive. In the UK, closed material proceedings were introduced to make it easier to adduce intelligence—that is, material that falls short of the necessary evidential standard—in civil proceedings. This meant that TPIMs could be imposed in lieu of a criminal prosecution being commenced. The same is true of the amendments to Division 104 of the Criminal Code, and thus they should, in theory, have resulted in an increase in the use of the control order regime. Instead, as is demonstrated in Chapter 2, what we have actually seen is a far greater reliance on prosecutions as a means of dealing with the foreign terrorist fighters phenomenon. This is so in spite of the inherent limitations of the criminal laws previously discussed. One conclusion that might be drawn from this is that closed material proceedings and special advocates were not as urgent and necessary an addition to the control order regime as the Australian Government had claimed.

3.3 Changes to the United Kingdom TPIMs Regime

In contrast to the numerous changes to Australia's control order regime, the UK Parliament has only amended the TPIMs Act once in the foreign terrorist fighters era.[105] In September 2014, the then Prime Minister, David Cameron, stated:

> [W]e need stronger powers to manage the risk posed by suspected extremists who are already in the United Kingdom. The Home Secretary can already impose terrorism prevention and investigation measures on security grounds, including overnight residence requirements and internet restrictions, but the intelligence agencies and the police believe they need stronger powers to impose further restrictions. . . . So we will introduce new powers to add to our existing terrorism prevention and investigation measures, including stronger locational constraints on suspects under TPIMs, either through enhanced use of exclusion zones or though [sic] relocation powers.[106]

Shortly thereafter, the then Home Secretary, Theresa May, asked the Independent Reviewer of Terrorism Legislation (IRTL), David Anderson, to conduct a review to inform precisely what amendments should be made to the system of TPIMs. In particular, he was asked whether 'the operational objectives for the management of TPIM subjects could be met through the sole use of exclusion zones' or whether 'some form of relocation power would be needed'.[107] At this point in time, the Home Secretary could not relocate any person subject to a TPIM unless they specifically agreed to it.

Anderson reported six days later, highlighting that whilst exclusion zones were 'useful in deterring TPIM subjects from travelling to prohibited areas or places, including for the purpose of harmful association', in the absence of relocation, they could 'do nothing to prevent a subject from meeting harmful associates on his home patch for the purposes of terrorist plotting, facilitating an abscond, or simply maintaining links and networks'.[108] He concluded that the 'power to relocate subjects away from their home areas would be of real practical assistance to the police and MI5'.[109] The focus on relocation was controversial. Under the control orders regime in the PTA, which was repealed by the TPIMs Act, the Home Secretary could impose any obligations considered necessary to prevent or restrict a person's involvement in terrorism-related activity. This power was virtually unlimited in scope and enabled the Home Secretary to, amongst other things, relocate controlees away from their usual place of residence. Such relocation was described by critics of the control orders regime as a form of 'internal exile'.[110] It was therefore intentionally excluded from the list of measures available to the

Home Secretary under the TPIMs Act when it was introduced in 2011 as part of the incoming Coalition Government's promised programme of security 'liberalisation'.[111]

The Counter-Terrorism and Security Act (CTS Act) implemented Anderson's recommendation to introduce a specific relocation power into the TPIMs regime. The power was inserted by amending the 'overnight residence measure' which the Home Secretary could impose as part of a TPIM. The amendment enables the Home Secretary to relocate TPIM subjects up to 200 miles away from their normal residence[112] or even further if the new premises are in an 'agreed locality'.[113] This is defined as a locality agreed upon by the Home Secretary and the individual subject to the TPIM.[114]

Three further amendments were made to the list of obligations, prohibitions, and restrictions which could be imposed by the Home Secretary under a TPIM. First, the Home Secretary could prohibit an individual from 'possessing offensive weapons, imitation firearms or explosives' or from 'making an application for a firearm certificate or a shot gun certificate'.[115] The second amendment was the introduction of an 'appointments measure'. Pursuant to this, the Home Secretary could require an individual to 'attend appointments with specified persons or persons of specified descriptions'.[116] This measure was designed with deradicalisation programmes in mind. Its introduction implemented recommendations made by Anderson in his annual report on TPIMs in March 2014.[117] Finally, the TPIMs Act was amended to make it an offence to contravene a travel restriction measure, irrespective of whether the subject of the TPIM had a 'reasonable excuse' for the contravention.[118] The penalty for contravening a travel restriction measure was increased from five to ten years imprisonment.[119]

The changes made by the CTS Act were rationalised by the UK Government as necessary in order 'to deal with the increased terrorist threat'.[120] Specifically:

> The Government's ability to disrupt individuals from travelling abroad to engage in terrorism-related and other serious or organised criminal activity has become increasingly important with developments in Syria and other parts of the world. We need to do more to disrupt individuals travelling from the UK to fight for terrorist organisations, and to manage those individuals who seek to return here.[121]

The Home Office highlighted the important role played by TPIMs in disrupting individuals 'with past or present involvement in terrorist related activity' from engaging in acts of terrorism in the UK.[122] It stated: 'TPIMs . . . give the Security Services and police powerful measures to help manage the risk these individuals pose'.[123] The Explanatory Notes to the CTS Bill further noted the need to 'strengthen existing arrangements for monitoring and controlling individuals involved in terrorism-related activity in the UK'.[124] The system of TPIMs as it operated in 2014 was regarded as inadequate to respond to the problem of foreign terrorist fighters because it 'does not currently allow TPIM subjects to be moved out of their "locality" and does not compel subjects to meet specified persons to contribute to their management'.[125] The benefits of requiring people subject to a TPIM to attend meetings was plainly stated:

> If the support is successful, TPIM subjects will be less likely to influence, plan and/or execute an attack. A terrorist attack can have a large impact on the UK, both in terms of the immediate impact, such as lives lost, damaged infrastructure and lost output, and longer term costs such as higher public anxiety.[126]

The UK Government did not simply claim that the amendments to the TPIMs regime outlined above were necessary. It also maintained that they were sufficiently urgent to require the legislation to be introduced using the parliamentary fast-track procedure.[127] Urgency has been a hallmark of lawmaking in the UK, as with many other countries, in the anti-terrorism context. Whilst there may be instances in which immediate legislative action is required in order to address a particular threat, a clear statement of justification should be demanded. This is because legislating in a climate of urgency carries inherent risks, in particular, that the human rights implications of the legislation and concerns about whether it will in fact be effective are glossed over. An examination of the very limited extent to which the amendments to the TPIMs Act have been relied upon to date reveals that the UK Government's claims of urgency were overblown.

Eight new TPIMs have been issued by the Home Secretary since the amendments entered into force on 12 February 2015.[128] Despite the UK Government's insistence that the new powers were urgent and necessary to deal with the foreign terrorist fighters phenomenon, there was no significant increase in the use of the TPIMs regime until 18 months after the amendments were enacted. Only two new TPIMs were issued in the first six months after the amendments were introduced.[129] It was only from June 2016 onwards that there was a spike in their use; six new TPIMs were issued in the three months ending 31 August 2016.[130] Two of those have since expired and, at time of writing, only six TPIMs remain in force.[131]

Each of the post-amendment TPIMs imposed the new relocation measure.[132] Most of the individuals subject to TPIMs were relocated to outside of London, so as to reduce their ability to abscond to participate in the Syrian and Iraqi conflicts.[133] Justice Mitting noted in the case of EB that 'the principle justification for the [relocation] measure is . . . that it reduces the likelihood that EB will abscond, leave the United Kingdom and resume terrorism-related activity abroad'.[134] He continued: 'It is significantly more difficult to abscond from the United Kingdom from a provincial city than from London'.[135] This appears to be borne out in practice; none of the eight people subject to a post-amendment TPIM have absconded. Although it is extremely difficult to prove causation, the relocation measure seems to have been effective in preventing people from travelling to participate in the Syrian and Iraqi conflicts. However, the critical test of the current TPIMs regime will come in mid-2018. This is when the six TPIMs currently in effect expire and the relocation measure ceases to restrict freedom of movement. At that point, it is possible that any or all of the six people subject to a TPIM may attempt to travel to the conflict zones. This outcome will be less likely if those individuals have been diverted away from the path of violent extremism during the course of their TPIM. This is where the appointments measures—also introduced by the CTS Act—become significant.

Five of the eight TPIMs are known to have included some form of an appointments measure.[136] Both EC and EG were required to engage 'with a case worker whose function is to moderate extremist views and to ensure that any tendency to criminality is avoided'.[137] Under an appointments measure, IM, JM, and LG were required to meet with an 'Intervention Provider'.[138] However, there have been mixed reviews of the practical utility of this amendment to the TPIMs regime. Justice Nicol noted that 'LG appears to have embraced the meetings with his [Intervention Provider]—Imam Shafi Chowdhury . . . with enthusiasm. He has had numerous meetings with Imam Chowdhury since they first met on 17th August 2016. Some of the meetings have lasted several hours'.[139] He was less optimistic about IM and JM's meetings: 'IM and JM have also been required to, and have, met with [Intervention Providers], although on a less frequent basis'.[140] Similarly, Justice Collins noted that a report of EC's meetings with a case worker was 'encouraging', however, it was 'too early to be satisfied that he has indeed renounced his extremist views'.[141] EG, on the other hand, was struggling to 'understand why he should eschew any extremism', despite attending meetings with a case worker on a weekly basis.[142] Insufficient time has lapsed since the introduction of the appointments measure to assess its success. As with the relocation measure, it is only when the current TPIMs expire in mid-2018 that the diversionary effects of the appointments measures will be able to be evaluated.

The third and final measure introduced into the TPIMs regime by the CTS Act was the prohibition on 'possessing offensive weapons, imitation firearms or explosives'.[143] This measure was included in the TPIM obligations imposed upon IM, JM, and LG.[144] There is no information available as to whether this measure was included in any of the other five TPIMs imposed in the foreign terrorist fighters era. It is also not particularly clear what this measure adds to the Government's counter-terrorism armoury. It is already a criminal offence in the UK to possess offensive weapons, firearms, and explosives without a certificate, and it is highly unlikely that anyone suspected of terrorism would be granted one. The only plausible use for this measure is to remove the need to prove the physical and mental elements of a firearms offence at trial. Breach of the conditions of a TPIM is a more straightforward offence to prove.

Unlike the Australian amendments to the control orders regime, the UK amendments *have* been relied upon by the authorities, albeit on only eight occasions and not on a regular basis until more than a year after they were introduced. This, in combination with two final amendments made by the CTS Act, points to a more restrained approach being taken by the UK Government to lawmaking in the anti-terrorism context than that shown by its Australian counterpart. The latter has—in both the criminal and hybrid civil-criminal contexts—demonstrated a willingness to regularly expand its legislative armoury in spite of there being no concrete evidence of necessity. What has been demonstrated by the UK Government, in contrast, is a greater level of reflexivity.

The first of these amendments was to raise the threshold for imposing a TPIM from 'reasonable belief' to the civil standard of 'on the balance of probabilities'.[145] According to the then Home Secretary, Theresa May, this change merely reflected existing practice. In a speech to the Royal United Services Institute (RUSI) shortly before the CTS Bill was introduced into the UK Parliament, she stated that: 'our analysis shows that every single TPIM issued so far would have passed this threshold'.[146] The other amendment narrowed the definition of 'terrorism-related activity' upon which the imposition of a TPIM was based. The effect of the amendment was to exclude conduct which merely:

> gives support or assistance to individuals who are known or believed by the individual concerned to be involved in conduct . . . which facilitates the commission, preparation or instigation of such acts, or which is intended to do so, [or] which gives encouragement to the commission, preparation or instigation of such acts, or which is intended to do so.[147]

This change again merely reflected existing practice. In his annual report on TPIMs in 2013, Anderson noted that '[t]he unnecessarily broad definition of terrorism-related activity . . . allows TPIMs to be imposed upon persons whose involvement with terrorism is highly peripheral',[148] and could be used 'against a person whose connection with an act of terrorism could be as remote as the giving of support to someone who gives encouragement to someone who prepares an act of terrorism'.[149] However, he added the caveat that 'they are not in practice imposed' in those circumstances:[150] 'TPIM subjects to date have all been believed to be more than just peripheral figures where terrorism is concerned'.[151]

3.4 Conclusions

Australia and the UK have adopted different approaches to amending their hybrid sanctions regimes to deal with the threat posed by foreign terrorist fighters. Over a period of two years, the Australian Federal Parliament enacted three laws which made substantial modifications to the control order regime. These included amendments to the grounds and terms on which a control order can be sought by the AFP and issued by the court, the lowering of the minimum age for control orders, and the introduction of a system of closed material proceedings and special advocates in control order hearings. In contrast, and in line with the trend highlighted in Chapter 2, the UK Parliament appeared remarkably restrained. However, the changes it made were no less controversial, in particular, the introduction of a relocation measure into the list of TPIM obligations. Despite claims by both the Australian and UK Governments that the amendments to their hybrid sanctions regimes were urgent and necessary, only four control orders and eight TPIMs have been issued since the amendments were introduced. The limited use of these measures raises considerable doubt over both their initial necessity as well as their effectiveness in practice.

The Australian control order regime as it existed in 2014 was already adequately targeted to the threat posed by foreign terrorist fighters. This is demonstrated by the fact that none of the four control orders issued in Australia relied upon the recent amendments. In fact, no orders have even been issued since the last piece of legislation amending the regime was enacted in 2016. Measures simply cannot be effective if they have not been used. This is not to suggest that there is no place for control orders in Australia's legislative framework—although this argument has frequently been made—but rather that the Government's claims as to the necessity and urgency of new measures needs to be subjected to greater scrutiny. The 'gaps' that the amendments to the control order regime were designed to fill have turned out not to be the chasms invoked by the Government.

The picture is slightly different in the UK. Even though only eight new TPIMs have been issued since the amendments to the TPIMs regime were introduced in early 2015, all eight have included the new relocation power, which the UK Government considers to be one of its strongest tools in preventing TPIM subjects from engaging in terrorism-related activity. The application of the relocation measure to the eight TPIM subjects may indeed have prevented them from absconding to engage in terrorism, either in the UK or abroad in the Syrian and Iraqi conflicts.

However, use is only one part of the story. Any assessment of a measure's effectiveness is reliant upon its ability to achieve its desired result. The amendments to both the Australian control order and UK TPIMs regimes were intended to prevent terrorism. The fact that there have been at least four (and arguably five) terrorist attacks inspired by Islamic extremism in Australia since the start of the Syrian and Iraqi conflicts, and four such attacks in the UK in 2017 alone, does not in and of itself mean that control orders and TPIMs have been ineffective. What it does show, however, is that the amendments made to both regimes since 2014 have not been able to capture the people who engaged in those attacks. At best, what can be said is that the four control orders in Australia and eight TPIMs in the UK stopped those particular individuals from engaging in terrorism for the duration of their orders.

The current threat from foreign terrorist fighters cannot be dealt with by hybrid sanctions alone. The 200 individuals under investigation in Australia for providing support to those involved in the Syrian and Iraqi conflicts, and the more than 20,000 people who have come to the attention of the UK authorities, cannot all be made subject to a control order or TPIM. For one, it would be prohibitively expensive and would not be a valuable or efficient use of the intelligence and security agencies in Australia and the UK. More importantly, however, is that not all of those individuals who have come to the attention of the authorities require such strict controls as would be imposed by control orders or TPIMs; they do not all pose the same level of threat. Hybrid sanctions should be relied upon only where the authorities have significant intelligence that the individual poses a threat to society, but insufficient evidence exists to prosecute them for a criminal offence. Where this is not the case, the Australian and UK authorities would be better served in attempting to stop the flow of human and financial resources to the Syrian and Iraqi conflicts by focusing upon early intervention strategies.

Notes

1 Andrew Ashworth and Lucia Zedner, *Preventive Justice* (Oxford: Oxford University Press, 2014) 181–91.
2 Ibid., 181.
3 See Tamara Tulich, 'Post-Sentence Preventive Detention and Extended Supervision of High Risk Offenders in New South Wales' (2015) 38 *University of New South Wales Law Journal* 823; Bernadette McSherry, 'Sex, Drugs and "Evil" Souls: The Growing Reliance on Preventive Detention Regimes' (2006) 32 *Monash University Law Review* 237.

4 Andrew Ashworth and Lucia Zedner, *Preventive Justice* (Oxford: Oxford University Press, 2014) 181–2.
5 Ibid., 184.
6 Prevention of Terrorism Act 2005 (UK). Control orders were created to replace the Home Secretary's power to indefinitely detain non-national suspected terrorists who could not otherwise be deported: ss 21–3 of the Anti-Terrorism, Crime and Security Act 2001 (UK). This power was found by the House of Lords to contravene the HRA: *A v Secretary of State for the Home Department* [2005] 2 AC 68.
7 Prevention of Terrorism Act 2005 s 1(3). A representative—but non-exhaustive—list of the types of restrictions that could be imposed was provided in s 1(4).
8 Ibid., s 2(1).
9 Ibid., s 9(4).
10 Criminal Code Act 1995 (Cth) div 104.
11 Terrorism Prevention and Investigation Measures Act 2011 (UK) s 1.
12 Criminal Code Act 1995 (Cth) s 104.5(3); Terrorism Prevention and Investigation Measures Act 2011 (UK) sch 1.
13 Criminal Code Act 1995 (Cth) s 104.16(1)(d); Terrorism Prevention and Investigation Measures Act 2011 (UK) s 5(1)(b).
14 Terrorism Prevention and Investigation Measures Act 2011 (UK) s 5(2).
15 Criminal Code Act 1995 (Cth) s 104.16(2).
16 Ibid., s 104.27.
17 Terrorism Prevention and Investigation Measures Act 2011 (UK) s 23(3).
18 Criminal Code Act 1995 (Cth) s 104.2–104.4.
19 Ibid., s 104.5.
20 Ibid., ss 104.5(1A), (1B).
21 Ibid., s 104.12A(4)(a).
22 Terrorism Prevention and Investigation Measures Act 2011 (UK) s 3.
23 Ibid., sch 4.
24 Ibid.
25 Ibid., sch 4 s 10.
26 Criminal Code Act 1995 (Cth) ss 104.2(3A), 104.5(2A), 104.12A(3), 104.23(3A). 'National security' is defined in s 8 of the NSIA as 'Australia's defence, security, international relations or law enforcement interests'. Section 17 of that Act states that '[a] disclosure of information is *likely to prejudice national security* if there is a real, and not merely a remote, possibility that the disclosure will prejudice national security' (emphasis in original).
27 Criminal Code Act 1995 (Cth) s 104.2(3A).
28 Ibid., s 104.5(2A).
29 Ibid., s 104.12A.
30 Ibid., s 104.23(3A).
31 Roger Gyles, 'Control Order Safeguards Part 2' (April 2016) xx.
32 Ibid.
33 Ibid., 11.
34 Explanatory Memorandum, Counter-Terrorism Legislation Amendment (Foreign Fighters) Bill 2014 (Cth) 2; Explanatory Memorandum, Counter-Terrorism Legislation Amendment Bill (No 1) 2014 (Cth) 1.
35 Explanatory Memorandum, Counter-Terrorism Legislation Amendment (Foreign Fighters) Bill 2014 (Cth) 2.

36 Explanatory Memorandum, Counter-Terrorism Legislation Amendment Bill (No 1) 2014 (Cth) 1.
37 Explanatory Memorandum, Counter-Terrorism Legislation Amendment (Foreign Fighters) Bill 2014 (Cth) 2.
38 Louise Hall, 'Terror Suspect Denied Bail, Will Challenge Control Order "in First Case of Its Kind"', *Sydney Morning Herald*, 12 February 2015 <www.smh.com.au/nsw/terror-suspect-denied-bail-will-challenge-control-order-in-first-case-of-its-kind-20150211-13ckyf.html>.
39 *R v MO (No 1)* [2016] NSWDC 144 [3].
40 *R v MO (No 2)* [2016] NSWDC 145 [7]–[8].
41 *Gaughan v BXO15* (Unreported, SYG3493/2014, Federal Circuit Court of Australia, Cameron J, 23 December 2015); *Gaughan v BXO15* (Unreported, SYG3493/2014, Federal Circuit Court of Australia, Cameron J, 18 September 2015).
42 *Gaughan v Naizmand* (Unreported, SYG562/2015, Federal Circuit Court of Australia, Driver J, 19 October 2015).
43 *Gaughan v Causevic (No 2)* [2016] FCCA 1693.
44 *Gaughan v Naizmand* (Unreported, SYG562/2015, Federal Circuit Court of Australia, Driver J, 30 November 2015).
45 'Ahmad Naizmand' on *Australian National Security Law* <https://ausnatsec.wordpress.com/ahmad-naizmand/>.
46 This was one of ten controls which had originally been placed on Naizmand: *Gaughan v Naizmand* (Unreported, SYG562/2015, Federal Circuit Court of Australia, Driver J, 19 October 2015) Interim Control Order sch 1.
47 *R v Naizmand* [2016] NSWSC 836 [6].
48 Ibid.
49 *R v Naizmand* [2017] NSWDC 4.
50 *Gaughan v Causevic* (Unreported, MLG2056/2015, Federal Circuit Court of Australia, Hartnett J, 10 September 2015) Interim Control Order.
51 *IMO an Application for a Preventative Detention Order in Respect of Causevic* (2015) 251 A Crim R 481.
52 Adam Cooper and Michael Bachelard, 'Anzac Day Terror Charge Against Melbourne Teen Harun Causevic Dropped', *The Age*, 25 August 2015 <www.theage.com.au/victoria/anzac-day-terror-charge-against-melbourne-teen-harun-causevic-dropped-20150825-gj6y5n.html>.
53 Calla Wahlquist, 'Tracking Device Removed from Teenager Formerly Linked to Anzac Day Terrorist Plot', *Guardian*, 8 July 2016 <www.theguardian.com/australia-news/2016/jul/08/tracking-device-removed-from-teenager-previously-linked-to-anzac-day-terror-plot>.
54 See Chapter 4 at 69.
55 The delay occurred because Causevic applied to transfer the control order confirmation hearing to the Federal Court of Australia. The application was denied: *Gaughan v Causevic* (2016) 309 FLR 135.
56 *Gaughan v Causevic (No 2)* [2016] FCCA 1693 [2].
57 Criminal Code Act 1995 (Cth) s 104.2(2)(a).
58 Explanatory Memorandum, Counter-Terrorism Legislation Amendment (Foreign Fighters) Bill 2014 (Cth) 123.
59 Ibid., 36.
60 Criminal Code Act 1995 (Cth) s 104.2(2).
61 Ibid., ss 104.2(2)(b), (c), (d).

62 Ibid., s 104.4(1)(c).
63 Ibid., s 104.1.
64 Commonwealth, *Parliamentary Debates*, House of Representatives, 1 December 2014, 13635 (Michael Keenan, Minister for Justice).
65 Commonwealth, *Parliamentary Debates*, Senate, 29 October 2014, 8163 (George Brandis, Attorney-General).
66 Commonwealth, *Parliamentary Debates*, House of Representatives, 1 December 2014, 13636 (Michael Keenan, Minister for Justice).
67 Commonwealth, *Parliamentary Debates*, Senate, 25 May 2017, 183–4 (Duncan Lewis, Director-General of Security).
68 *Gaughan v Naizmand* (Unreported, SYG562/2015, Federal Circuit Court of Australia, Driver J, 19 October 2015) Interim Control Order [3]; *Gaughan v Causevic* (Unreported, MLG2056/2015, Federal Circuit Court of Australia, Hartnett J, 10 September 2015) Interim Control Order sch 2 [11]; *R v MO (No 1)* [2016] NSWDC 144 [1].
69 *Gaughan v Naizmand* (Unreported, SYG562/2015, 19 October 2015) Interim Control Order [3].
70 *Gaughan v Causevic* (Unreported, MLG2056/2015, Federal Circuit Court of Australia, Hartnett J, 10 September 2015) Interim Control Order sch 2 [11].
71 *Gaughan v Causevic (No 2)* [2016] FCCA 1693 [4].
72 Ibid; *Gaughan v Naizmand* (Unreported, SYG562/2015, Federal Circuit Court of Australia, Driver J, 19 October 2015) Interim Control Order [3].
73 *R v MO (No 1)* [2016] NSWDC 144 [1].
74 James Renwick, 'Control Orders and Preventative Detention Orders' (September 2017) 58.
75 Ibid., 66.
76 Ibid.
77 See Chapter 2 at 14.
78 *Criminal Code Act 1995* (Cth) s 104.2(3).
79 Ibid., s 104.4(2)(b).
80 Ibid., s 104.5(1) Note 2.
81 The use of children by Islamic State has been one of the defining features of the organisation. See Francesca Capone, 'Child Soldiers: The Expanding Practice of Minors Recruited to Become Foreign Fighters', in Andrea de Guttry, Francesca Capone, and Christophe Paulussen (eds), *Foreign Fighters Under International Law and Beyond* (The Hague: TMC Asser Press, 2016); John Horgan et al., 'From Cubs to Lions: A Six Stage Model of Child Socialization into the Islamic State' (2017) 40 *Studies in Conflict and Terrorism* 645.
82 Explanatory Memorandum, Counter-Terrorism Legislation Amendment Bill (No 1) 2016 (Cth) 19–20.
83 Commonwealth, *Parliamentary Debates*, Senate, 12 November 2015, 8426 (George Brandis, Attorney-General).
84 Paul Farrell, 'Judge Confirms First Control Order in More than Eight Years on Man, 20', *Guardian*, 1 December 2015 <www.theguardian.com/australia-news/2015/dec/01/judge-confirms-first-control-order-in-over-eight-years-on-man-20>; Megan Levy, 'Boy, 12, Monitored in Connection with Suspected Terrorist Activity: AFP', *Sydney Morning Herald*, 15 October 2015 <www.smh.com.au/national/boy-12-monitored-in-connection-with-suspected-terrorist-activity-afp-20151014-gk9cyy.html>; *Gaughan v Naizmand* (Unreported, SYG562/2015, Federal Circuit Court of Australia, Driver J, 19 October 2015).

85 James Renwick, 'Control Orders and Preventative Detention Orders' (September 2017) 66.

86 See Chapter 4 at 78–9.

87 Katharine Murphy, 'Ten-Year-Olds Could Be Held Without Charge Under New Terrorism Laws', *Guardian*, 5 October 2017 <www.theguardian.com/australia-news/2017/oct/05/ten-year-olds-held-without-charge-new-terrorism-laws>.

88 'Plane Attack Suspects "Put Bomb in Barbie"', *The Australian*, 22 August 2017 <www.theaustralian.com.au/national-affairs/national-security/plane-attack-suspects-planted-bomb-in-barbie-doll/news-story/53ed1a83566b3f355d2ba37a 54655a44>.

89 See Chapter 2 at 32–3.

90 James Renwick, 'Control Orders and Preventative Detention Orders' (September 2017) 66.

91 Ibid.

92 National Security Information (Criminal and Civil Proceedings) Act 2004 (Cth) ss 38J(2)–(4).

93 Ibid., ss 38J(2)(d)–(e), (3)(c)–(d), (4)(b)–(c).

94 Ibid., s 38J(1)(c).

95 Roger Gyles, 'Control Order Safeguards—(INSLM Report) Special Advocates and the Counter-Terrorism Legislation Amendment Bill (No 1) 2015' (January 2016) 10.

96 COAG, 'Review of Counter-Terrorism Legislation Report' (2013) 59–60.

97 National Security Information (Criminal and Civil Proceedings) Act 2004 (Cth) s 38PA(1).

98 Ibid., s 38PC(3).

99 Ibid., s 38PC(1).

100 Ibid., s 38PB.

101 Ibid., s 38PE.

102 Ibid., s 38PF.

103 Ibid., s 38PD.

104 Explanatory Memorandum, Counter-Terrorism Legislation (Amendment) Bill (No 1) 2016 (Cth) 29.

105 Counter-Terrorism and Security Act 2015 (UK) pt 2.

106 United Kingdom, *Parliamentary Debates*, House of Commons, 1 September 2014, vol. 585, col. 26 (David Cameron, Prime Minister).

107 David Anderson, *Relocation, Relocation, Relocation* (Independent Reviewer of Terrorism Legislation, 25 November 2014) <https://terrorismlegislation reviewer.independent.gov.uk/relocation-relocation-relocation/>.

108 Ibid.

109 Ibid.

110 Helen Fenwick and Gavin Phillipson, 'Covert Derogations and Judicial Deference: Redefining Liberty and Due Process Rights in Counterterrorism Law and Beyond' (2011) 56 *McGill Law Journal* 863, 877–85.

111 HM Government, 'The Coalition: Our Programme for Government' (20 May 2010) 24. See also David Anderson, 'The Terrorism Acts in 2012' (July 2013) 12. Despite aiming to 'liberalise' the control order regime, the TPIM Act retained many of its controversial features. For analysis of the differences between the two regimes, see Adrian Hunt, 'From Control Orders to TPIMs: Variations on a Number of Themes in British Legal Responses to Terrorism'

(2014) 62 *Crime, Law and Social Change* 289; Clive Walker and Alexander Horne, 'The Terrorism Prevention and Investigation Measures Act 2011: One Thing But Not Much the Other?' [2012] *Criminal Law Review* 421.
112 Counter-Terrorism and Security Act 2015 (UK) s 16(2).
113 Ibid., s 16(3).
114 Terrorism Prevention and Investigation Measures Act 2011 (UK) sch 1 s 1(5).
115 Counter-Terrorism and Security Act 2015 (UK) s 18.
116 Ibid., s 19.
117 David Anderson, 'Terrorism Prevention and Investigation Measures in 2013' (March 2014) 50–4.
118 Counter-Terrorism and Security Act 2015 (UK) s 17(3).
119 Ibid., s 17(4).
120 Home Office, 'Counter-Terrorism and Security Bill—Terrorism Prevention and Investigation Measures' (Impact Assessment No HO0146, 18 November 2014) 1 <www.gov.uk/government/uploads/system/uploads/attachment_data/file/540546/Terrorism_Prevention_and_Investigation_Measures_IA.pdf>.
121 Ibid., 4.
122 Ibid., 1.
123 Ibid., 4.
124 Explanatory Notes, Counter-Terrorism and Security Bill 2014 HC Bill (2014–15) 10–11. See also ibid., 5.
125 Explanatory Notes, Counter-Terrorism and Security Bill 2014 HC Bill (2014–15) 10–11.
126 Home Office, 'Counter-Terrorism and Security Bill—Terrorism Prevention and Investigation Measures' (Impact Assessment No HO0146, 18 November 2014) 9 <www.gov.uk/government/uploads/system/uploads/attachment_data/file/540546/Terrorism_Prevention_and_Investigation_Measures_IA.pdf>.
127 Ibid., 6.
128 Six of these eight persons are known as EB, EC, EG, IM, JM, and LG. Two TPIM subjects are currently unknown. Their TPIMs were issued between 1 June 2015 and 31 August 2015 and between 1 September 2016 and 30 November 2016.
129 EB was issued with a TPIM on 21 April 2015: United Kingdom, *Parliamentary Debates*, House of Commons, 11 June 2015, HCWS26 (Theresa May, Home Secretary). A second TPIM was issued against an unknown person in the reporting period from 1 June 2015 to 31 August 2015: United Kingdom, *Parliamentary Debates*, House of Commons, 17 September 2015, HCWS206 (Theresa May, Home Secretary).
130 United Kingdom, *Parliamentary Debates*, House of Commons, 26 October 2016, HCWS220 (Amber Rudd, Home Secretary). The TPIM issued between 1 June 2015 and 31 August 2015 expired in this period.
131 United Kingdom, *Parliamentary Debates*, House of Commons, 16 October 2017, HCWS173 (Amber Rudd, Home Secretary).
132 Information available from the Home Secretary's Written Ministerial Statements on TPIMs. See United Kingdom, *Parliamentary Debates*, 10 December 2015, HCWS382 (Theresa May, Home Secretary); United Kingdom, *Parliamentary Debates*, House of Commons, 19 July 2017, HCWS173 (Amber Rudd, Home Secretary).
133 *Secretary of State for the Home Department v EC* [2017] EWHC 795 (Admin); *Secretary of State for the Home Department v EB* [2016] EWHC 1970 (Admin); *Secretary of State for the Home Department v LG* [2017] EWHC

1529 (Admin). These cases involve the six known TPIM subjects: EB, EC, EG, IM, JM, and LG.

134 *Secretary of State for the Home Department v EB* [2016] EWHC 1970 (Admin) [38].

135 Ibid., [39].

136 *Secretary of State for the Home Department v EC* [2017] EWHC 795 (Admin); *Secretary of State for the Home Department v LG* [2017] EWHC 1529 (Admin). No information is available as to whether the other three TPIMs also included an appointments measure.

137 *Secretary of State for the Home Department v EC* [2017] EWHC 795 (Admin) [35].

138 *Secretary of State for the Home Department v LG* [2017] EWHC 1529 (Admin) [32].

139 Ibid.

140 Ibid.

141 *Secretary of State for the Home Department v EC* [2017] EWHC 795 (Admin) [35].

142 Ibid., [46].

143 Counter-Terrorism and Security Act 2015 (UK) s 18, inserting para 6A into sch 1 of the Terrorism Prevention and Investigation Measures Act 2011 (UK).

144 *Secretary of State for the Home Department v LG* [2017] EWHC 1529 (Admin) [32].

145 Counter-Terrorism and Security Act 2015 (UK) s 20(1).

146 Theresa May, 'Home Secretary Theresa May on Counter-Terrorism' (Speech delivered at RUSI, London, 24 November 2014) <www.gov.uk/government/speeches/home-secretary-theresa-may-on-counter-terrorism>.

147 Counter-Terrorism and Security Act 2015 (UK) s 20(2).

148 David Anderson, 'Terrorism Prevention and Investigation Measures in 2013' (March 2014) 4–5.

149 Ibid., 49.

150 Ibid., 4–5.

151 Ibid., 49.

4 Immigration and Citizenship

4.1 Introduction

One of the defining features of State counter-terrorism responses to the foreign terrorist fighters phenomenon has been the enactment and amendment of immigration and citizenship laws. This is not the first time that such laws have been used as counter-terrorism tools. For example, following the September 11 terrorist attacks, the UK enacted measures allowing the Home Secretary to indefinitely detain non-national terrorist suspects who could not be deported.[1] These measures reflected the concern that States were most at threat from terrorism conducted by foreign citizens, as had been the case with the September 11 hijackers. As the threat of terrorism evolved in the first decade of the twenty-first century, both the Australian and UK Governments became concerned about the possibility of their own citizens engaging in terrorism. In line with this change, the focus of anti-terrorism legislation shifted away from immigration and citizenship laws, and towards measures directed at controlling the activities of citizens suspected of involvement in domestic terrorism.[2]

The advent of the foreign terrorist fighters phenomenon in the second decade of the twenty-first century has seen a return to the use of immigration and citizenship measures, albeit this time predominantly targeting citizens (as opposed to foreign nationals). These measures have focused on preventing citizens from attempting to join the Syrian and Iraqi conflicts as well as preventing those who are abroad and suspected of supporting the activities of Islamic State and its affiliates from returning home. The key concern for governments is the increased capacity of returned foreign terrorist fighters to engage in terrorism on domestic soil because of experience obtained in Syria and Iraq. This chapter examines Australia and the UK's legislative attempts to prevent potential foreign terrorist fighters from departing the relevant jurisdiction, as well as the legislative measures introduced to prevent suspected foreign terrorist fighters from returning home.

This chapter differs from the preceding chapters. The secrecy surrounding immigration and citizenship decisions means that there is limited information on the use of these powers. Therefore, this analysis relies more heavily on a combination of official reports, which tend to provide statistics in aggregate form and without context, as well as media reports. The lack of detailed information means that much of the analysis remains somewhat abstract, making it difficult to come to a decisive conclusion about the effectiveness of certain immigration or citizenship tools.

4.2 Preventing Potential Foreign Terrorist Fighters From Departing

The primary means by which the Australian and UK Parliaments have sought to prevent suspected foreign terrorist fighters from travelling overseas is through the enactment of new legislation and the amendment of existing legislation relating to passports and travel documents. In addition, both Australia and the UK have introduced measures enhancing the ability of customs and border protection agencies to prevent aspiring foreign terrorist fighters from leaving the country.

4.2.1 *Passports and Travel Documents*

Prior to the start of the Syrian and Iraqi conflicts, the Australian Government already had powers to cancel or refuse to issue a passport on national security grounds. Relevantly, this included situations where a 'competent authority'[3] believed on reasonable grounds that the person was: prevented from foreign travel by a court order, bail condition, parole condition, or similar under either domestic or foreign law; the subject of a domestic or foreign arrest warrant in respect of a serious offence; or, likely to engage in harmful conduct either in Australia or overseas—such as prejudicing the security of a country or endangering the safety or freedoms of other persons—if allowed to travel.[4] In 2014, the Foreign Fighters Act amended the Australian Passports Act 2005 (Cth) to give the Minister for Foreign Affairs the additional power to *suspend* passports and travel documents for 14 days at the request of the Director-General of Security.[5] Once suspended, an officer could demand that the passport be surrendered.[6] A complementary power relating to the surrender of foreign passports was also introduced in 2014.[7] Failure to surrender is a criminal offence.[8]

According to the Explanatory Memorandum to the Foreign Fighters Bill, the primary purpose of the amendments was to 'enhance the Australian Government's capacity to take proactive, swift and proportionate action to mitigate security risks relating to Australians travelling overseas'.[9] It described the new power to suspend travel documents as 'a discretionary power to take temporary action'.[10] This is reflected in the low evidentiary threshold imposed by the legislation. Before making a request, the Director-General of Security must simply have reasonable grounds to suspect that 'the person *may* leave Australia to engage in conduct that *might* prejudice the security of Australia or a foreign country'.[11] This low threshold—and hence the relative ease with which a suspension order can be made—is somewhat mitigated by the 14-day time limit. A suspension order cannot be renewed at the end of that period unless new information is uncovered by the Australian Security Intelligence Organisation (ASIO).[12] The only further option would be to request the cancellation of the person's travel documents, which would be more difficult because it requires the existence of reasonable grounds to suspect that the person 'would be likely' to engage in such conduct.[13] Nevertheless, a 14-day limit is, on the whole, a lacklustre safeguard. There is technically nothing preventing ASIO from repeatedly suspending a person's passport on the basis of different or new information at the end of each 14-day period.

These new powers were not uncontroversial. The Explanatory Memorandum to the Foreign Fighters Bill noted that the 'changes implement several recommendations of the INSLM's fourth annual report'.[14] However, in that report, the Independent National Security Legislation Monitor (INSLM), Bret Walker, proposed the implementation of rolling 48-hour suspensions up to a total maximum of seven days only.[15] In its report on the Bill, the Senate Standing Committee for the Scrutiny of Bills drew attention to this 'significant difference'.[16] The Committee stated:

> The only justification [provided by the government] for this difference is that this is 'necessary to ensure the practical utility of the suspension period with regard to both the security and passports operating environment'. It appears that neither the explanatory memorandum nor the statement of compatibility provide further elaboration of this point.[17]

Prior to making a recommendation on this issue, the Senate Standing Committee for the Scrutiny of Bills sought the Attorney-General, George Brandis's, 'advice as to the rationale for requiring a 14 day suspension period'.[18] Brandis responded that a shorter period would have been insufficient to allow ASIO and the Minister for Foreign Affairs to assess whether to cancel the relevant person's travel documents.[19] He continued: 'A period of 14 days seeks to strike the right balance between the rights of an individual to travel and the need to ensure Australia's national security'.[20] In its final report, the Committee noted this response, but left the 'question of whether the proposed approach is appropriate to the Senate as a whole'.[21] The Parliamentary Joint Committee on Human Rights (PJCHR) was marginally less sanguine about the matter. It noted the absence of empirical support for the assertion that 14 days was 'necessary to ensure the practical utility of the suspension period'.[22] The PJCHR was also concerned about the effect of the passport suspension power on freedom of movement. The Explanatory Memorandum to the Foreign Fighters Bill justified the temporary restriction of a person's right to travel as consistent with the International Covenant on Civil and Political Rights (ICCPR),[23] stating that the power to suspend passports was provided for by law and was 'reasonable and necessary' in order to protect national security.[24] However, the PJCHR criticised these 'general assertions' as insufficient, contrasting them against the INSLM's 'evidence-based rationale' for 48-hour rolling suspension periods.[25] In making an adverse assessment of the proposal, it also noted the restriction of administrative review[26] and exclusion of judicial review in relation to suspension orders,[27] and the capacity to avoid giving notice of a refusal or cancellation.[28] These measures decrease transparency and make it far more difficult for an individual to challenge the suspension of their passport.

The suspension power was passed by the Australian Federal Parliament with minimal amendments in 2014. In its first two years of operation, 33 passports were suspended by the Minister for Foreign Affairs, Julie Bishop.[29] In March 2017, it was reported that an additional three passports had been suspended.[30] Alongside the new suspension power, the Minister has increasingly used the pre-existing powers to cancel or refuse a passport on national security grounds. From February 2014 to May 2017, 137 passports were cancelled, nearly two and a half times the figure for the previous three year period.[31] The utility of powers to cancel passports to prevent the exit of aspiring foreign terrorist fighters is apparent from the case of Amin Mohamed, a New Zealand citizen who was prevented by the AFP from boarding a plane from Brisbane to Syria after the cancellation of his passport by New Zealand authorities.[32] This does not mean passport cancellations are an infallible method of preventing an aspiring foreign terrorist fighter's exit. Despite the cancellation of his passport, convicted terrorist and foreign terrorist fighter Khaled Sharrouf was able to leave the country without alerting the authorities by travelling on his brother's passport.[33] UK citizen Siddhartha Dhar also managed to travel to Syria, after leaving London by coach with his wife and children whilst on bail awaiting trial for terrorism offences.[34] His bail conditions included the surrender of his travel documents and prohibition of international travel. However, the surrender was not immediately enforced at the time of his release on bail. A letter demanding the surrender of 'all travel documents at Charing Cross police station' was instead sent to his home address six weeks after he had already left with his family for Syria.

In addition to the ability of individuals to circumvent the suspension or cancellation of their passports, there is the possibility that the passport powers may prove counter-productive in certain situations. This is because an aspiring foreign terrorist fighter may become aware that they are under investigation and, in place of travelling overseas, seek to undertake hostile acts domestically. For example, Sevdet Besim was found guilty of planning to attack a police officer during the 2015 Anzac Day parade in Melbourne. The purpose, in his words, was to 'make sure the dogs remember this as well as their fallen heroes'.[35] Besim had attempted to apply for an Australian passport in March 2014, but was informed that his application was under investigation.[36] It seems that this refusal to grant him a passport—whilst successfully preventing his exit—was the impetus for his plan to conduct a domestic terrorist attack. In a martyrdom note written shortly before he was arrested, Besim said:

> At first i wanted nothing else but to leave this country and live in the Islamic State, however after many complications with my passport i realised this could not be done. . . . So i started to prepare myself for my attack against the enemies of Islam.[37]

The impact of being refused a passport was also reflected in online conversations between Besim and a 14-year-old boy from the UK who acted as his mentor. The conversations, uncovered by UK counter-terrorism forces one week before the Anzac Day parade, formed the basis of the prosecution case against Besim. Besim told the 14-year-old: 'I was supposed to leave jan this year to go to Dubai i had it all thought out, then when my passport went under investigation i knew what i had to do'.[38] The boy—whose name has never been released—was arrested by UK authorities on the same day as Besim and ultimately sentenced to life imprisonment for inciting terrorism overseas.[39]

The passport issue did not arise in the 14-year-old's case, since he neither possessed nor applied for a passport.[40] Nevertheless, in 2015, the UK Parliament introduced mechanisms similar to those in Australia for the temporary suspension of travel documents. Schedule 1 of the Counter-Terrorism and Security (CTS) Act allows a constable to temporarily retain a person's passport and travel documents at a port or border.[41] The constable must have reasonable grounds to suspect that the person is attempting to exit the country to engage in terrorism-related activities abroad. This suspicion can be formed based on prior intelligence or at the scene, and need not be limited to a suspicion that the person will engage in front-line fighting.[42] Once this threshold is met, the constable has the power to demand, search for, inspect, and seize passports and other travel documents, such as airline tickets. In making this demand, the person must be informed of the suspicion, but need not be informed of the grounds on which it is based.[43] If the person resists or refuses to cooperate with the constable's demands, the border detention power under Schedule 7 of the TA 2000—which will be discussed in more detail below—comes into operation.

A passport seized under Schedule 1 can be retained for up to 14 days without judicial approval,[44] and up to another 16 days at the discretion of the courts.[45] The CTS Act states that this may occur whilst: the Home Secretary considers whether to cancel the individual's passport; consideration is given to charging the individual with an offence or making them subject to an order such as a TPIM discussed in Chapter 3; or, 'steps are taken to carry out' those actions.[46]

The 14-day retention can be authorised by a senior police officer on the same reasonable grounds for suspicion as is required for initially seizing the passport.[47] Once the passport has been retained for 72 hours, a police officer must review whether this retention is 'flawed'.[48] If so, the passport must be returned to its owner. Whilst ostensibly legislated to prevent abuses of power, the failure to define 'flawed' means that the review process is inherently subjective and a negative outcome would be virtually impossible to challenge. If a judicial extension is sought, the person subject to the passport retention is given the opportunity to make representations to the court and can be granted legal aid.[49] However, at the request of police, and on the basis that 'national security would be put at risk', sensitive information can be withheld from both that person and their legal representative.[50] In an attempt to mitigate the harshness of these provisions, the relevant Home Office Code of Practice states that if a judicially approved extension is applied for, the suspect is entitled to ask for, and be provided with, written reasons for the exercise of the power.[51] These reasons are to be 'as full as possible but without prejudicing national security'.[52]

At the culmination of the hearing, the judicial authority is required to grant an extension if it is satisfied that the investigation of the individual and their passport is being dealt with 'diligently and expeditiously'.[53] However, the judicial authority cannot have any regard to the merits of the investigation.[54] The exclusion of substantive considerations and the ability to conduct closed proceedings are disproportionate.[55] There is no minimum level of disclosure, which diminishes the value of even the procedural judicial assessment of the investigation. Furthermore, although this power may be reviewed by the Independent Reviewer of Terrorism Legislation (IRTL),[56] there is no sunset clause or mandated legislative re-evaluation of the power's operation.

In the absence of sufficient procedural and substantive safeguards, these powers raise concerns about the inevitable restriction of personal freedom resulting from passport seizure and retention. The restriction on a person's freedom of movement was justified in the Explanatory Notes to the CTS Bill because of the necessity and urgency of 'bring[ing] in further measures to strengthen border and transport security measures' by disrupting imminent travel.[57] Yet, the measures are only of limited value in preventing the international movement of aspiring foreign terrorist fighters. At the end of the 30-day period, unless sufficient information has been gathered to support a passport cancellation or the pursuit of criminal or civil orders, the passport will be returned and the aspiring foreign terrorist fighter will be free to travel. If officers wish to seize and retain the same individual's passport again within the next six months for a period of more than five days, the court must be satisfied that there are exceptional circumstances justifying such action.[58] Other commentary has noted that this gap is not addressed in the legislation and, therefore, the authorities have been forced to develop innovative approaches. For example, the Family Division of the High Court has been used to prevent minors from exiting the UK.[59] This has involved the courts either subjecting parents to orders involving passport removal, injunctions, monitoring and electronic tagging, or making the children wards of the court to prevent their removal from the country.[60]

The UK Government reported that passports were retained 24 times between February and December 2015.[61] Official numbers for 2016 are not available, but reports indicate that from January to July 2017, another 40 passports were cancelled or suspended.[62] These numbers are not statistically insignificant; however, it is important to bear in mind that the powers are neither infallible nor comprehensive. As in Australia, foreign terrorist fighters have exited the UK on relatives' passports.[63] The resort to family law to prevent the international movement of the children of aspiring foreign terrorist fighters highlights another practical gap in the legislation. Considered alongside the lack of procedural and substantive safeguards available to those subject to a passport suspension or cancellation, the actual necessity of the measures comes into question.

Prior to the enactment of the CTS Act in 2015, the only legislative power to seize and retain passports for counter-terrorism purposes was via a Foreign Travel Restriction Order (FTRO).[64] Such an order may be used to restrict travel to specified countries or to prohibit foreign travel completely, and involves the surrender of the person's passport.[65] On its face, this would seem to play a role in preventing aspiring foreign terrorist fighters from travelling overseas. However, an FTRO is in fact only useful in very limited circumstances. In particular, the person must have been convicted of a terrorism-related crime and have served their sentence.[66] Once released, two further conditions must be met. The person must be subject to 'notification requirements',[67] and their behaviour since release must make an FTRO necessary in order to prevent them from engaging in terrorist activity abroad.[68] Even then, enforcement can be problematic as the case of *R v Brooks and Keeler* demonstrates.[69] Following a 2008 conviction for inciting and funding terrorism,

Brooks was subject to an FTRO which required him to inform police of any intention to leave the UK. Nevertheless, both he and Keeler left for Turkey in the back of a lorry, without passports and without informing police.[70] They were ultimately deported from Hungary back to the UK, but not due to the efficacy of the FTRO. This is one of only a few cases on the use of FTROs in the context of the foreign terrorist fighters phenomenon and, as noted by the IRTL, David Anderson, there is 'an absence of recently published information on these powers'.[71] As a result, it is difficult to gauge their proportionality or efficacy, other than noting that they may be of some use in very specific circumstances.

In addition to the suspension of passports and imposition of FTROs, the Home Secretary has the power to issue, cancel, or refuse UK passports under the royal prerogative. This is an important point of distinction between the two jurisdictions covered by this book. Powers with respect to passports are conferred upon the Australian Government by the Australian Passports Act 2005 (Cth). Due to the comprehensive way in which this Act addresses passport law—'specially empower[ing] the Crown to do the same' as under the royal prerogative[72]—any residual prerogative power which may have been retained by the Australian Government in relation to passports and travel has been effectively curtailed.[73] Therefore, unlike in the UK, action in Australia in relation to travel documents is limited to that expressed in statute.

Use of the royal prerogative so far as passports and travel documents are concerned is highly discretionary. It applies if a person is: subject to a UK arrest warrant; wanted by police on suspicion of committing a serious crime; subject to a court order, bail conditions, or other order by the EU or UN which involves the imposition of travel restrictions or prohibition of possession of a passport; or, if it is in the public interest.[74] This final criterion is unique to the UK; there is no equivalent in the Australian legislative framework. The Home Secretary can refuse or cancel a passport if he or she believes that the past, present, or potential future activities of the person are so 'undesirable' that their possession of a passport would be contrary to the public interest.[75] Further, whilst the primary purpose of this power in relation to terrorism is the prevention of overseas travel by aspiring foreign terrorist fighters, according to the former Home Secretary, Theresa May, passports can be cancelled or refused 'whether overseas travel was or was not a critical factor'.[76] Rather, refusal or cancellation may be based on the individual's 'past, present or proposed activities—actual or suspected', even where it does not relate to the potential for international travel.[77] It is highly doubtful whether use of the prerogative power in circumstances that seem unrelated to an individual's intention to travel overseas is either necessary or rational. This is especially so considering how actual or perceived injustices—arguably including the severe restriction of the freedom of movement of an individual who has no intention of becoming a foreign terrorist fighter—can cause distrust of government, and be a further driver for radicalisation.[78]

The prerogative power was unsuccessfully challenged in *Re (XH) v Secretary of State for the Home Department*.[79] The appellants were suspected of intending to travel overseas to engage in terrorism-related conduct. As a result, their UK passports were cancelled. The appellants tried to argue that the use of the royal prerogative power in this context was unlawful. They relied on the general principle that statute can override and supersede the royal prerogative power (as indeed it has done in the Australian context), positing that the introduction of Terrorism Prevention and Investigation Measures (TPIMs) had done so in the context of foreign travel restrictions to prevent terrorism-related conduct. The Court of Appeal rejected this argument. It held that there was no parliamentary intent to exclude the royal prerogative and nor were the two sets of powers unable to co-exist. They were of different scope and application; namely, the prerogative power applied to a wider set of circumstances and its removal would generate 'an obvious area of public risk and lack of security'.[80] Indeed, even though TPIMs are in place, the application of the royal prerogative power has increased markedly in comparison to historic levels of use. In the nearly 30 years between 1947 and 1976, the power was used a total of 16 times.[81] In contrast, it was used 24 times in 2014 and 23 times in 2015.[82] Statistics from 2016 and 2017 are not yet available.

4.2.2 Customs and Border Protection

Since 2014, customs and border protection officials in Australia and the UK have been given broader powers to detain aspiring foreign terrorist fighters, and hence prevent their departure. In Australia, the Foreign Fighters Act amended the Customs Act 1901 (Cth) in 2014 to make it easier to detain people attempting to travel out of—or back into—Australia. According to the Revised Explanatory Memorandum, these amendments were directed at 'individuals thought to be threats to Australia's national security leaving the country'.[83] They were emphasised as not only preventing Australians from engaging in hostile activity as foreign terrorist fighters—conduct which negatively impacts Australia and its allies' reputations and interests—but also as limiting 'the threat of returning foreign fighters'.[84] Prior to the 2014 changes, Australian border officials were able to detain travellers suspected of having committed, or being in the process of committing, a 'serious Commonwealth offence', that is, a federal offence punishable by imprisonment for at least three years. The Foreign Fighters Act significantly expanded this definition and its application under the Customs Act to include offences punishable by imprisonment for at least one year.[85] It also lowered the threshold for detention to require merely reasonable grounds to suspect that the person *intends* to commit such an offence.[86] Furthermore, the Foreign Fighters Act introduced a new basis on which border officials can detain travellers: where the officer is satisfied on reasonable grounds that the person is, or is likely to be, involved in activities which threaten the security of Australia or a foreign country.[87] This latter basis for detention is very broad. It would seem to cover all of the possible circumstances surrounding the travel of foreign terrorist fighters, rendering the expanded definition of a 'serious Commonwealth offence' obsolete and unnecessary for that purpose.[88]

These amendments have attracted considerable criticism. The PJCHR was concerned that it was not possible to undertake a proper proportionality analysis because the amending Bill did not have a 'sufficiently well-defined objective'.[89] This is highlighted by the lack of connection between the expanded definition of a 'serious Commonwealth offence' and the foreign terrorist fighters phenomenon.[90] Pre-2014, the definition was limited to certain categories of crime which provided for a maximum period of imprisonment of at least three years.[91] All specific terrorism offences satisfy those requirements. Advocating terrorism, for example, carries up to five years imprisonment,[92] whilst the maximum penalty for recruitment of a foreign terrorist fighter[93] and presence in a declared zone[94] is ten years imprisonment. Even the offence of associating with a member of a terrorist organisation carries a maximum term of three years.[95]

In effect, the expanded definition covers many minor offences, the vast majority of which are unrelated to terrorism or foreign terrorist fighters, under the auspices of a '*targeted* response to the threat posed by foreign fighters'.[96] The Senate Standing Committee for the Scrutiny of Bills therefore questioned the necessity of expanding the definition to cover crimes punishable by one year imprisonment.[97] The Parliamentary Joint Committee on Intelligence and Security (PJCIS) recommended removing it from the amending Bill.[98] The only justification for the change is set out in the Statement of Compatibility with human rights accompanying the Foreign Fighters Bill.[99] It claims that the expanded detention powers are appropriate because they are only triggered by the 'gravest threats' to Australia, namely, those which threaten national security or can result in one or more years imprisonment. In response to the remarks of the Senate Standing Committee for the Scrutiny of Bills, the Attorney-General, George Brandis, noted that there were offences carrying shorter terms which could prove very useful to customs officials suspicious of an outbound passenger.[100] He referred specifically to the offence of using a passport issued to someone else.[101] Even taking this into account, it still seems excessive to broaden the scope of 'serious Commonwealth offences' to all offences with a maximum penalty of one or more years imprisonment. It would have been a more tailored and targeted approach to have merely expanded the previous definition to include specific additional offences, such as the passport offence mentioned by Brandis, as well as criminal offences with maximum imprisonment of three years or more.

The UK has also used customs and border protection legislation to address the exit of aspiring foreign terrorist fighters, although, unlike in Australia, recent amendments have focused more on the seizure and retention of travel documents than on the expansion of detention powers. Prior to 2014, UK police and border officials already had extensive powers to prevent outbound travel. Under Schedule 7 of the Terrorism Act 2000 (TA 2000), an examining police officer is able to question, search, and detain an individual for the purpose of ascertaining whether they are or have been involved in terrorist activity. Whilst the examining officer must believe that the individual's presence at the border or port is connected with their entering or leaving the UK, there is no need for prior knowledge, belief, or even suspicion about the individual's involvement in terrorism.[102] This power has been buttressed with the introduction of the Anti-Social Behaviour, Crime and Police Act 2014 (UK). Schedule 8 of this Act gives border officials at any port the power to search for and take possession of a person's travel documents for up to seven days. The border officials simply need to suspect that the documents are invalid, that is, that they have been cancelled, or are fake or altered. Unless invalidity is confirmed, the travel documents must be returned.

Despite the added legislative tools, use of these powers has consistently decreased. In 2015–16, 28,083 travellers were examined across the UK, a fall of 19 percent from the previous year.[103] The former IRTL, David Anderson, speculated that this downward trend was due to the improved capture of passenger data and targeting techniques.[104] These factors may help explain why, even though use has decreased, there has, at the same time, been an increase in the number of detentions and arrests stemming from examination of travellers at border areas. The number of detentions increased 39 percent from 2014–15 to 2015–16, whilst arrest numbers increased nearly 50 percent.[105] Nevertheless, the proportion of arrests to examinations is still nominal. Of the 28,083 travellers examined in 2015–16, only 58 were arrested.[106] Indeed, the House of Commons Home Affairs Committee noted that the 'vast majority' of those referred by border officials to specialised counter-terrorism forces were not of interest.[107]

This is not necessarily indicative of a lack of effectiveness. As noted by Anderson and the Supreme Court, stops at borders and ports are a way of dissuading the 'young, nervous or peripheral' of terrorist networks.[108] Further, each questioning is part of a 'jigsaw' approach to security work which can 'yield vital results beyond the significance initially apparent from any single piece of information'.[109] Anderson has also observed that so long as the searches and examinations are non-discriminatory,[110] 'non-confrontational . . .

and no longer than necessary',[111] they can be a proportionate way of simultaneously improving intelligence, disrupting inter-state movement, and assisting in the conviction of terrorists. However, there is no concrete information about whether or not the laws have achieved these positive results. The measures' potential positives also need to be considered in a context where approximately 850 people have travelled from the UK to the Syrian and Iraqi conflicts.[112] Whilst the number of Britons exiting the country has decreased in recent years, it is not at the moment ascertainable whether this trend stems from the deterrent effect of customs and border legislation, or simply because such travel is less appealing now that the Islamic State caliphate is in decline.

4.3   Preventing Suspected Foreign Terrorist Fighters From Returning

There are three categories of persons whose return the Australian and UK Governments have sought to restrict: foreign nationals; foreign terrorist fighters who hold either sole or dual citizenship; and, foreign terrorist fighters' families. The first of these categories has proved the easiest to deal with, even though neither Australia nor the UK have laws specifically targeted at excluding foreign nationals with links to terrorism.

4.3.1   Foreign Nationals

In Australia, ordinary visa rules are generally flexible enough to prevent foreign nationals suspected of being foreign terrorist fighters from entering the country. This is because the 'character test' must be satisfied. If it is not, the Minister for Immigration or their delegate has the power to refuse or cancel a visa.[113] The character test will not be met if: the individual is suspected of involvement with a declared terrorist organisation; there is a significant risk that they will incite discord or represent some danger to the Australian community; or, they are subject to an adverse security assessment.[114] According to the Department of Immigration, the Minister may also take into account whether: the individual holds 'extremist views such as the view that violence is a legitimate means of political expression'; the individual poses 'some threat' to Australians; and, their presence would be contrary in some other way to the public interest or Australia's foreign policy interests.[115] Whilst not all visitors to Australia require a formal visa,[116] all are subject to this character test.

A further mechanism is the 'emergency visa cancellation' enacted in the Foreign Fighters Act.[117] This mandates cancellation of a visa where ASIO reasonably suspects that the visa-holder currently outside of Australia might be a risk—whether directly or indirectly—to security. It is intended to cover circumstances where ASIO's information is 'not sufficient . . . to meet existing legal thresholds' required to cancel a visa,[118] and provides ASIO with a 28-day window in which to prove that the visa-holder is actually a risk.[119] If this cannot be done, the visa cancellation is revoked.[120]

The extent to which these visa mechanisms have been used in respect of foreign nationals suspected of involvement in the Syrian and Iraqi conflicts is unclear, due to the secrecy surrounding immigration decisions. However, an example of their use prior to those conflicts was Willie Brigitte, a French citizen married to an Australian woman. In 2003, he was deported to France, where he was convicted of criminal conspiracy in relation to terrorism offences. A spokesperson for the Department of Immigration stated that he would be denied re-entry on the basis of the character test.[121]

Unlike Australia, the UK's power stems from royal prerogative rather than statute, and there are relatively recent statistics on its use. A 2017 report stated that 69 people had been excluded from the UK between 11 May 2010 and 31 December 2015 on national security grounds, with 25 of those exclusions occurring in 2015 alone.[122] As for the scope of the prerogative power, Sir William Blackstone, writing in the eighteenth century, adopted a broad interpretation, noting that foreigners were 'liable to be sent home whenever the king sees occasion'.[123] The test currently adopted by the Home Office is slightly more specific: whether the individual's presence would not be 'conducive to the public good'. The Home Secretary's decision must be 'reasonable, consistent and proportionate', based on the evidence available.[124] As is often the case with aspects of the prerogative power, there is little detail of the standards that must be met. For example, it is unclear what evidence is required to render an exclusion 'reasonable, consistent and proportionate'. Evidently, the test was met in the case of conservative Saudi Arabian Sunni cleric, Mohammed al-Arifi. Al-Arifi, who has over 19 million followers on Twitter, gave a number of sermons while visiting the UK. In early 2014, the Home Office decided to exclude him from returning to the UK again, on the basis that he represented 'a threat to our society' and sought to 'subvert our shared values'.[125]

A different test currently applies to the exclusion of European Economic Area nationals and their families.[126] Exclusion can only be sought on the basis that the individual poses a genuine, present, and sufficiently serious threat affecting 'one of the fundamental interests of society'.[127] This includes the physical security of the population.[128] The test for seriousness is fact-specific;[129] however, it can be met where the individual has previously committed a serious criminal offence and there is a high level of risk that they will re-offend,[130] or where there is repeated commission of minor offences.[131]

4.3.2   *Citizens and Deprivation of Citizenship*

It is far more difficult—legally, morally, and practically—to exclude citizens. The Australian Minister for Foreign Affairs, Julie Bishop, stated that the Government is taking 'every step [it] can' to prevent foreign terrorist fighters from returning to Australia.[132] The UK Prime Minister, Theresa May, also urged fellow G7 members to collaborate and cooperate in stopping and prosecuting returning foreign terrorist fighters before they reach their home countries.[133] In line with this, both countries have introduced new legislation to facilitate the exclusion of citizen foreign terrorist fighters, either through citizenship-stripping powers or the temporary exclusion of citizens from the country. However, the laws are not proving as effective as was initially hoped. Nor are they in line with the dictates of international comity and the international cooperation that the global threat of terrorism warrants. Laws that strip citizenship or exclude nationals from one country simply serve to export or displace terrorism to another.

Prior to the Syrian and Iraqi conflicts, the legal position in Australia was that a citizen could not be excluded. This was so regardless of whether they were 'desirable'[134] or held a valid Australian passport.[135] Citizenship deprivation, and thus lawful exclusion, could only occur in very specific situations, for example, if an individual had naturalised by way of fraud.[136] However, in 2015, the Australian Federal Parliament amended the Citizenship Act to enable citizenship revocation for terrorism-related conduct.[137] This was in response to concerns about returning foreign terrorist fighters, and was heavily influenced by contemporary UK developments. The UK—which will be examined later in this chapter—has a much longer history of citizenship revocation than Australia. In the lead-up to the Australian amendments, the UK extended its citizenship revocation regime even further. The influence of this is apparent in the Minister for Immigration, Peter Dutton's, comment in the Australian Federal Parliament that '[t]he government was guided by what has happened in the United Kingdom, where [the Immigration Act 2014 (UK)] . . . allowed for dual citizens to be stripped of their British citizenship'.[138] The ensuing Australian amendments introduced three new avenues by which a dual citizen—that is, someone who possesses citizenship of Australia as well as another country—over the age of 14 could lose their Australian citizenship.

The first avenue is by engaging in conduct that 'repudiates' one's allegiance to Australia. The scope of 'repudiating' conduct clearly captures foreign terrorist fighters. It includes, but is not limited to, recruiting for, or training with, a terrorist organisation, and engaging in a terrorist act or hostile activities overseas.[139] In addition to the conduct requirement, a motivational element must also be satisfied. That is, the conduct must be engaged in with the intention of: advancing 'a political, religious or ideological cause'; and, coercing or intimidating the government—or part thereof—of the Commonwealth, a State, Territory, or a foreign country, or intimidating all or part of the public.[140] This intention element applies to each form of 'repudiating' conduct, including the foreign incursions and recruitment offences. To make it easier to prove, intention can be deemed by virtue of an individual's membership of, or cooperation with, a terrorist organisation.[141] The law purports to work automatically, that is, at the moment the conduct and intention arise simultaneously, the individual's citizenship is considered to be renounced.[142] It is only if the Minister for Immigration decides to use their non-compellable discretion that an individual may be exempted from the provision's application.[143] This first avenue of citizenship deprivation is aimed at citizens who are abroad. The provision only applies to an individual who has engaged in the relevant conduct overseas or has managed to leave Australia after having committed a terrorism-related act before they were tried.[144]

The second means of citizenship deprivation is similar in three respects. It also purports to automatically revoke an individual's citizenship, is limited to conduct occurring outside of Australia and is subject to a non-compellable discretion of the Minister to exempt the individual.[145] It arises where an individual serves or fights for a 'declared terrorist organisation'. A declared terrorist organisation is defined as an organisation which the Minister determines on reasonable grounds is involved in perpetrating or advocating terrorist acts, whether indirectly or directly, and which is opposed to Australia's interests and values such that being in its service is inconsistent with any allegiance to Australia.[146] Notably, there is no intention requirement. In response to concerns regarding the breadth of this provision, exceptions were provided for situations where the conduct is unintentional, engaged in under duress, or part of 'neutral and independent' humanitarian aid.[147]

The third avenue by which a dual citizen can be deprived of their Australian citizenship arises if they are convicted of one or more of specified terrorism offences and sentenced to at least six years imprisonment.[148] In such circumstances, the Minister is empowered to make a written determination on their citizenship status. The Minister must consider whether the individual's conduct shows a repudiation of allegiance to Australia as well as applying a public interest test. The latter takes into account a broad range of factors such as the severity of the conduct, the threat the individual poses to the Australian community, their age (and if they are a minor, the best interests of the child), any connection to their other country of citizenship, Australia's international relations, and other matters of public interest that may be relevant.[149]

It would be difficult to challenge the revocation of citizenship under any of these avenues. There is no merits review,[150] ostensibly for the reason that merits review would not be appropriate in light of the Minister's personal powers of exemption.[151] Furthermore, there is limited scope for judicial review.[152] This is for three reasons. The first is the lack of any obligation to inform the individual of the grounds upon which their citizenship was revoked.[153] Second, the Minister's power to exempt a person from the provisions' application is personal and discretionary, and cannot be compelled in any circumstances by a third party.[154] Third, the first two avenues of citizenship loss purport to be self-executing. That is, they apply of their own accord without any executive or judicial decision-making. This is problematic for judicial review as there is no specific decision to review.[155]

The existence of the Citizenship Loss Board highlights the lack of accountability in the Australian citizenship revocation regime. This Board is responsible for reviewing automatic revocations of citizenship. In effect, it is the decision-making body behind the first two aforementioned means of citizenship deprivation. The Board considers whether an individual's conduct meets the criteria for citizenship revocation, and then makes recommendations to the Minister as to how to exercise his or her discretion to exempt a person from the regime's effect.[156] This makes it a very powerful body. However, the Citizenship Act makes no mention of its role. There are no rules as to how it functions or what evidence it takes into account, and its members are neither elected parliamentarians nor members of the judiciary. This is significant because the Australian Government justified the Minister's non-compellable and personal discretion by reference to his status as an elected representative.[157] Furthermore, the fact that the Board makes a decision as to the relevant individual's conduct and makes a following recommendation clearly undermines the idea that the law is self-executing. Nevertheless, the minutes of the Board's first meeting, obtained under a Freedom of Information request, show that the Board is confident that it merely provides advice and is not 'a decision-making body'.[158]

Not only are there accountability problems, but the new citizenship laws have also been of limited utility. To date, they have only been used once, in early 2017, to deprive Khaled Sharrouf of his Australian citizenship.[159] This is despite the fact that—as at September 2015—18 Australians had been identified as potential targets for citizenship revocation.[160] The failure to revoke citizenship on more occasions seems to be due, at least in part, to the inherent difficulties in proving that the relevant individual holds dual citizenship. To do so often requires the cooperation of the country of second citizenship. In Sharrouf's case, his other country of citizenship, Lebanon, cooperated with the Australian Government.[161] However, in many instances, the other country may not be willing to cooperate, particularly if they are also planning on revoking citizenship, or simply do not wish to deal with the individual. Outside the specific context of terrorism, a 2010 study by the Yale Centre for the Study of Globalisation found that a key challenge faced by the

US when deporting unwanted immigrants was the lack of cooperation from their home countries.[162] This was acknowledged in 2015 by Sarah Saldana, the then director of US Immigration and Customs Enforcement,[163] and it apparently continues to pose problems for the US Government.[164] Similar challenges have arisen with the EU's attempts to deport unsuccessful asylum applicants to their home countries, including Pakistan[165] and Afghanistan.[166] Significant challenges exist even when the deportee never had citizenship of the deporting country.

It is widely recognised that citizenship revocation and deportation (or exclusion) of a citizen is problematic. In 2016, the former IRTL, David Anderson, stated:

> There is something of a mismatch between the popular perception that citizenship stripping enables or equates to banishment . . . and the reality, acknowledged in part by the Government . . . that legal or practical reasons will tend to prevent the removal (or make it impossible to resist the return) of a single national whose UK citizenship has been taken away.[167]

Whilst this comment was made in the context of the revocation of citizenship from UK sole citizens, which will be discussed in more detail below, it is also applicable to the Australian provisions relating to dual citizens. The challenge this poses to the efficacy of the Australian revocation regime is demonstrated by the Minister for Immigration, Peter Dutton's, decision in 2017 to review the measures with a view to amendment.[168] Reports indicate that amendments would be aimed at: the need to prove dual citizenship; the need for the individual to have fought with a 'declared terrorist organisation' (which only includes Islamic State and Jabhat al-Nusra at this point);[169] and, the lack of retrospective application of the law. This means that evidence from prior to May 2016, when the law came into force, could not be used to support citizenship revocation. However, further legislation is not a solution. Whilst some of the practical difficulties associated with depriving foreign terrorist fighters of their citizenship could be overcome, for example, by lowering the threshold or relaxing the rules of evidence, this would not address the problem of securing the cooperation of the individual's other country of citizenship. Further, as will be discussed later in this chapter, the realities of global terror in a digital world means that excluding an individual from their home country is not effective in preventing terror attacks. This is the fundamental deficiency with any citizenship revocation regime.

As noted earlier, there is a longer history of citizenship revocation in the UK than in Australia. Most relevantly to the foreign terrorist fighters phenomenon, the British Nationality Act 1948 (UK), as enacted almost 70 years ago, enabled the revocation of citizenship from a 'disloyal or disaffected' naturalised citizen where continued citizenship would not be 'conducive to the public good'.[170] Naturalisation refers to the process by which a person becomes a citizen through long-term residency in the UK (as opposed to by birth or descent). This regime was expanded first in response to the September 11 terrorist attacks and subsequently to the July 2005 London bombings through the enactment of the Nationality, Immigration and Asylum Act 2002 (UK) and the Immigration, Asylum and Nationality Act 2006 (UK) respectively. The combined effect of these two Acts is to make all citizens—not merely those who have been naturalised—potentially subject to citizenship revocation where it would be 'conducive to the public good'.[171] There is no need to show that the individual is 'disloyal or disaffected' or has committed a relevant criminal offence, as had been required under the 1948 Act. This shift in the application of revocation laws in the UK reflected the then Prime Minister, Tony Blair's, comment that the 'rules of the game are changing'.[172] However, at the time, one important safeguard was left in place: citizenship could not be revoked on this ground where it would make the individual stateless.[173] This meant that, in effect, the measures could only be applied to dual citizens.

Terrorism falls squarely within the citizenship-stripping powers. The UK Government has explained that it considers revocation to be appropriate in responding to war crimes, serious organised crime, the protection of the UK and its allies' national security, and in response to 'unacceptable behaviours'.[174] 'National security' in this context encompasses terrorism threats,[175] cyber security,[176] the UK's global influence[177] and the vague notion of 'promoting our prosperity'.[178] The concept of 'unacceptable behaviours' was clarified in a statement by the then Home Secretary, Charles Clarke, on 24 August 2005.[179] It includes, but is not limited to, any expression (written or oral, domestic or abroad) that glorifies or justifies terrorist violence, seeks to provoke others to commit terrorist acts or other serious criminal acts, or fosters hatred that could result in violence between communities in the UK.[180]

The gap left by the citizenship revocation regimes after 2006—albeit one that is arguably both desirable and appropriate—was that revocation cannot occur where statelessness would result. Two high-profile cases highlighted this. The first concerned radical cleric, Abu Hamza, who was a naturalised UK citizen born in Egypt. In 2003, his UK citizenship was revoked on the ground that he was believed to have acted against the vital interests of the UK.[181] This decision was successfully appealed to the Special Immigration Appeals Commission (SIAC) in 2010. Hamza argued that the revocation left him stateless because he had previously been deprived of his Egyptian citizenship.[182] The issue of statelessness also arose in relation to Hilal Al-Jedda, an Iraqi citizen who sought asylum in the UK in 1992.[183] In 2000, he obtained UK citizenship, and pursuant to Iraqi law, his citizenship of that country lapsed.[184] After travelling to Iraq in 2004, Al-Jedda was arrested by US forces. He was later placed in British custody in Iraq and held without charge for over three years on suspicion of membership of a terrorist group. Prior to his release in December 2007, the then Home Secretary, Jacqui Smith, notified him that he may be deprived of his citizenship.[185] However, since it could not be shown that Al-Jedda was a national of another country at the time of the declaration, the Supreme Court unanimously held that the revocation was unlawful and that his citizenship should be restored.[186]

The Immigration Act 2014 (UK) was enacted by the UK Parliament to prevent a repeat of these situations in the context of the foreign terrorist fighters phenomenon.[187] The Explanatory Notes to the Immigration Bill stated: 'Following the Supreme Court judgment in *Al-Jedda*, the Bill will amend this power by also allowing naturalised persons to be deprived of their citizenship . . . even where to do so may render them stateless'.[188] The Minister for Security and Immigration, James Brokenshire, defended the measure, stating that the provisions sought to safeguard national security by plugging the gap highlighted in the *Al-Jedda* case.[189] Indeed, following these 2014 amendments—and three weeks after the Supreme Court judgment invalidating the first revocation—the Home Secretary revoked Al-Jedda's citizenship for a second, and thus far successful, time.[190]

Under the amended Act, a naturalised citizen can be made stateless if two prerequisites are satisfied. First, the Home Secretary must consider revocation to be 'conducive to the public good' on the basis that the individual has acted in a manner which is 'seriously prejudicial to the vital interests' of the UK.[191] Such conduct is envisaged as 'covering those involved in terrorism or espionage or those who take up arms against the British or allied forces'.[192] Second, the Home Secretary must have reasonable grounds to believe that the individual will be able to become a national of another country.[193] The legislation does not clarify the level of certainty required. However, statements by counsel for the Home Secretary in the *Al-Jedda* case are instructive. Although the 2014 amendments did not apply to the case, counsel asked the Court to find in the Home Secretary's favour on the basis that Al-Jedda could have applied for restoration of Iraqi citizenship after the loss of his UK citizenship, would have been able to re-obtain this citizenship, and hence would not be made stateless. This is essentially the same test as that in the 2014 amendments: that there are reasonable grounds to believe that the individual will be able to become a national of another country. The Court pressed counsel on the scope of their submission, asking whether 'a Jewish person's right to obtain Israeli nationality or a wife's right to obtain the nationality of her husband' would be sufficient.[194] Counsel went on to explain that the argument did not extend past the individual re-obtaining a previously held citizenship.[195] It is likely that the current legislative test has a similar scope.

Citizenship revocation is subject to notice and appeal provisions,[196] although no judicial approval of the Home Secretary's initial notice of revocation is required.[197] Since 2004, an appeal of citizenship deprivation has been 'non-suspensive'.[198] This means that the individual can be deprived of their citizenship and deported whilst an appeal is ongoing, immediately removing the foreign terrorist fighter—as a deemed security risk—from UK soil. If the individual's appeal is successful, the deprivation is held to have no effect[199] and citizenship is thus reinstated.[200] However, due to the use of Temporary Exclusion Orders (TEOs) discussed below, reinstatement of citizenship does not necessarily mean that a deportee will be able to return to the UK.

As the then Home Secretary, Theresa May, recognised, 'under international law, no country is allowed' to make a person stateless.[201] Nevertheless, the UK Government has defended the legality of its citizenship revocation provisions. For example, it has argued that although the UK ratified the 1961 UN Convention on the Reduction of Statelessness, it is entitled to retain its pre-existing power under the British Nationality Act 1948 (UK) to deprive someone of their citizenship for conduct 'seriously prejudicial to the vital interests of the state'.[202] The UK Government has also repeatedly expressed how seriously it takes the power to make a citizen stateless.[203] Introducing the provisions to the House of Commons in January 2014, May stated that she recognised citizenship deprivation as 'one of the most serious sanctions a state can take against a person and it is therefore not an issue that I take lightly'.[204]

In fact, the UK Government appears to have taken the issue so seriously that the power has never been used. It had not been used by the time a review of the provisions was published on 21 April 2016,[205] and it does not seem to have been used since. This is likely because of the practical difficulties involved in exercising this power. Not only must the Home Secretary have reasonable grounds to believe that the individual can obtain citizenship from another country, but the problem of deportation arises. If a person is made stateless whilst in the UK, they would likely be unable to leave or be deported to another country. As noted by the former IRTL, David Anderson, the UK Government itself has recognised that in such circumstances the individual 'could be given limited leave to remain in the UK, so that they were not left in a legal limbo'.[206]

In contrast, powers to revoke the citizenship of *dual* citizens in the UK have taken on a new life in response to the foreign terrorist fighters phenomenon. These powers are used not only on citizens within the UK, but also to strip citizenship from foreign terrorist fighters who are already abroad, thus preventing their return to the UK. From 2006 to 2010, a total of three citizenship deprivation orders were made under the 'conducive to the public good' ground.[207] In comparison, during Theresa May's tenure as Home Secretary, 33 citizenship deprivation orders were made on this basis.[208] More than half of these occurred from 2013 to 2014.[209] In the year and a half from January 2016 to July 2017, it was reported that another 80 revocations occurred (although it is not clear on what grounds).[210]

In addition to citizenship revocation, the Home Secretary often simultaneously uses the prerogative power to exclude the now foreign national, thus ensuring they cannot return to the UK on another passport.[211] *K2 v United Kingdom* is an example of how this works in practice.[212] In 2010, a citizenship deprivation order was served on K2 due to suspected involvement in terrorism-related activity in Somalia.[213] K2 unsuccessfully challenged this order. One of the arguments he raised related to his inability to return to the UK to pursue an appeal. He claimed that whilst abroad, he feared his communications would be intercepted by local counter-terrorism authorities, meaning that he could not properly make his case. The European Court of Human Rights disagreed, stating that the UK was not obliged under the European Convention on Human Rights (ECHR) to allow an individual who has been deprived of their UK citizenship to return in order to pursue an appeal.[214]

Another practical consideration which affects the utility of citizenship revocation is the mismatch between the purported effect of revocation as a protective measure and the realities of global terrorism. Regardless of where revocation occurs, domestically or abroad, it ultimately results in a person suspected or convicted of terrorism-related conduct being free. This creates 'a policy of catch and release'.[215] It leaves people in places where they can do more harm, and means that the government washes its hands of responsibility for its citizens. This is contrary to obligations imposed upon UN Member States. Nearly 40 United Nations Security Council (UNSC) Resolutions in relation to terrorism have been passed since the September 11 terrorist attacks. Depriving a foreign terrorist fighter of citizenship breaches at least four key aspects of these UNSC Resolutions: criminal prosecution of terrorists; prevention of terrorists' international movement; action in accordance with international human rights obligations; and, cooperation with other countries in dealing with terror threats, rather than evasion of responsibility in a manner contrary to the collective efforts of States to decrease the global threat of terrorism.[216] Each of these is critical to dealing effectively with the threat of foreign terrorist fighters.

For example, if a foreign terrorist fighter has their citizenship revoked and is left overseas, there is no guarantee that another country will arrest and charge them. The chances of this are even less if the individual is in a conflict zone. Unless the individual is killed, their movement is relatively uninhibited, allowing them to continue to engage in terrorism-related activity. This does not interdict the risk posed by this individual. Deprivation of citizenship in such circumstances does not dismantle the threat, but merely displaces it to a different jurisdiction. Whilst this may be politically convenient, it is logically incoherent. It encourages a 'dangerous delusion' that once a suspect individual is overseas, they can no longer do any harm to a State or its people.[217] This may also diminish domestic incentive to directly deal with the issue. Whilst it would be more difficult, it would not be impossible for an excluded foreign terrorist fighter to plan an attack on their home country or one of their home country's allies.[218] The 14-year-old boy who mentored Besim demonstrates the capacity for individuals to be directly involved in terror plots on the other side of the world.[219]

Such measures also do little so far as derailing Islamic State and other terrorist organisations are concerned. The treatment of foreign terrorist fighters who went to Afghanistan in the 1970s and 1980s is a case in point Many were prevented from returning to their home countries at the end of that conflict.[220] This did not solve the problem as these individuals instead turned to professional international jihadism, fighting in Algeria, Bosnia, Sudan, and Yemen. These excluded foreign terrorist fighters, under the leadership of Osama bin-Laden, ultimately formed the basis of Al-Qaida.[221] Indeed, concern over similar developments was raised at a fast-tracked summit in July 2017 of six Southeast Asian countries, including Australia, regarding the growth of pro-Islamic State forces in the Philippines and the ongoing battle for the city of Marawi.[222]

UNSC Resolutions complicate the use of citizenship revocation for terrorism-related conduct in another way. Both the Australian and UK Governments have tried to rely, sometimes successfully and at other times not, on UNSC Resolutions to justify their counter-terrorism laws and actions. For example, the Australian Government invoked Resolution 1373[223] to defend the constitutional validity of its interim control order scheme in the High Court case of *Thomas v Mowbray* in 2007.[224] In *R (Al-Jedda) v Secretary of State for Defence*, the UK Government invoked Resolution 1546 (and subsequent resolutions),[225] arguing that the legal regime established pursuant to these Resolutions qualified the rights in Article 5(1) of the ECHR.[226] It is hypocritical for countries to rely on these Resolutions in such circumstances and then to disregard them in relation to other legislative and executive developments.

4.4 Citizens and Temporary Exclusion

Despite the citizenship deprivation measures discussed above, the reality is that Australia and the UK cannot revoke the citizenship of all of their foreign terrorist fighter citizens, because many of those individuals are not dual citizens or do not have the ability to acquire a second citizenship. Therefore, in 2015, the UK created a new regime designed to temporarily exclude people falling into that category. There is no Australian equivalent to this and nor are there any plans at present to establish such a regime.

A TEO can be imposed on an individual if five conditions are met: (a) the Home Secretary must reasonably suspect 'that the individual is, or has been, involved in terrorism-related activity outside' the UK; (b) they must reasonably consider that it is necessary to impose a TEO to protect the public from a risk of terrorism; (c) they must reasonably consider that the individual is outside the UK when the order is imposed; (d) they must either have the prior permission of the court to impose an order or must reasonably consider that the case's urgency requires a TEO without judicial permission; and, (e) the individual must have the right of abode in the UK.[227] Once issued, the TEO invalidates the person's UK passport, thus preventing their return to the UK, unless it is either 'in accordance with a permit to return issued by the [Home Secretary]' or 'the result of the individual's deportation to the United Kingdom'.[228] A permit to return gives the individual permission to return to the UK, but may specify a number of conditions, including the time, manner, and location of re-entry.[229] Once the suspected foreign terrorist fighter has returned to the UK, the Home Secretary may impose a number of obligations on the individual, including a requirement to report to a police station, notify the police of their place of residence, and to attend appointments with specified persons.[230] It is an offence, punishable by a term of up to five years imprisonment, to contravene the terms of a TEO.[231]

In a statement to the UK Parliament on 1 September 2014, the then Prime Minister, David Cameron, outlined the threat posed by the return of foreign terrorist fighters and the Government's plans to counter it. He gave the example of 'a British citizen, who says that he wants to come back to Britain in order to wreak havoc in our country and who has pledged allegiance to another state'.[232] It was 'abhorrent', he said, 'that people who declare their allegiance elsewhere can return to the United Kingdom and pose a threat to our national security'.[233] The remedy was plain: 'what we need is a targeted, discretionary power to allow us to exclude British nationals from the UK'.[234]

Cameron's proposed power to 'exclude' UK citizens suspected of being foreign terrorist fighters was—like the revocation of citizenship from sole citizens of the UK—described as essential in order to fill 'a gap' in the Government's existing counter-terrorism toolkit. However, within two months, the proposal had been watered down to a system of 'managed return'.[235]

In outlining the draft legislation, the then Home Secretary, Theresa May, stated that:

> [T]he Bill will create a statutory Temporary Exclusion Order to control the return to the UK of a British citizen suspected of involvement in terrorism-related activity abroad . . . the message to British nationals participating in terrorism overseas is clear: you will only be allowed to come home on our terms.[236]

UK citizens would not be permanently excluded from the UK as had originally been proposed. Instead, they retained the right to return but could only do so with the knowledge and assistance of the UK authorities. The reasons for this shift in approach were not disclosed. The formal right to abode in the UK is based on statute—rather than being constitutionally entrenched—and is therefore susceptible to amendment.[237] However, one possible reason is the difficulties faced by the UK Government in finding a mechanism, consistent with international legal obligations, to actually *exclude* its citizens. Guy Goodwin-Gill has commented that even in its watered-down form, the TEO regime is 'likely incompatible with the duties which the State owes to its citizen, with the rights of other States, and with the obligation of the UK to prosecute certain offences (for which concerted international action is required)'.[238]

The development of the TEO regime also demonstrates the problems associated with trying to place political rhetoric on a statutory footing. The rhetoric was of exclusion, that is, banning UK citizens suspected of being foreign terrorist fighters from returning to the UK. The former IRTL, David Anderson, called this proposal 'an announcement waiting for a policy'.[239] He explained:

> Although it was announced on 1 September in terms that emphasised the need to exclude British nationals from their own country, I suspect it pretty soon became evident that neither legally nor practically was that going to work. So what we now have is a power that, although it entitled exclusion orders or temporary exclusion orders, in reality it is much closer to managed return or controlled return, which are two phrases that the Home Secretary used.[240]

In enacting the TEO legislation, the UK Parliament's core concern was that the return of individuals who had participated in the Syrian and Iraqi conflicts would 'pose a threat to our national security'.[241] Similarly to the introduction of TPIMs discussed in Chapter 3, the UK Government claimed the TEO legislation was necessary to fill a capabilities gap, and urgent enough to justify using the parliamentary fast-track procedure. The Explanatory Notes to the Bill justified this, referencing the seriousness of the threat and stating that TEOs

> would enable the law enforcement and intelligence agencies to disrupt and control the return to the UK of British citizens who have travelled abroad to engage in terrorism-related activity, and place requirements on them once returned, in order to manage the threat they pose at that point.

Despite this, there had been only one confirmed TEO as of May 2017.[242] Reports in July 2017 suggest that the Home Office has made 'several' more since then.[243] Regardless, this represents a minute proportion of the approximately 400 individuals who have returned to the UK from the Syrian and Iraqi conflicts.[244] It is not known how many of those have returned since the enactment of the CTS Act.[245] What is clear, however, is that in that same period, only one of the terrorist attacks carried out on UK soil has been perpetrated by a returned foreign terrorist fighter: the detonation of a bomb at the Manchester Arena by Salman Abedi, who had recently returned to the UK from Libya. Indeed, this attack appears to be an exception to the general trend. According to David Anderson: 'There were . . . no deaths or injuries from terrorism in Great Britain during 2015, unless one counts the injuries sustained by Lyle Zimmerman at Leytonstone tube station in London in December'.[246] The man convicted of attempted murder in that attack claimed that it was 'for [his] Syrian brothers', but he had not himself travelled to participate in the conflict, or been directed by any terrorist organisation.[247] Nor did anyone die in 2016 as a result of foreign terrorist fighter-related terrorism in the UK, although Labour parliamentarian, Jo Cox, was killed in June that year in a politically motivated attack linked to the far right and the referendum on the UK's membership of the EU.[248] There is also no evidence to suggest that any of the plots that were successfully disrupted during 2015 and the first half of 2016 involved returned foreign terrorist fighters.[249]

Whilst it is difficult to quantify, it is arguable that the existence of the TEO powers has had a deterrent effect, by preventing potential foreign terrorist fighters from leaving the UK in the first place or stopping them from attempting to return. However, on the whole, it makes little practical sense for the UK to rely on the law as a deterrent for those abroad from seeking to return home. The imposition of a TEO does not require the foreign terrorist fighter to already be attempting to return, nor does it need to be served personally on them.[250] The Home Secretary has the option to give notice by recorded delivery to the suspected foreign terrorist fighter's postal address or last known postal address, or to their representative.[251] If their 'whereabouts are not known' and 'no address is available for correspondence', 'the notice shall be deemed to have been given when the Home Secretary enters a record of the above circumstances and places the signed notice on the relevant file'.[252] In many of these circumstances, the suspected foreign terrorist fighter may have no knowledge that they are in fact subject to a TEO until they attempt to use their UK passport to travel. There is thus no obvious utility in using the TEO powers merely as a deterrent.

When introducing the power to Parliament, both the then Prime Minister, David Cameron, and Home Secretary, Theresa May highlighted that this was a targeted power designed to ensure the safety and security of the UK and prevent terrorism on home soil. On 1 September 2014, Cameron noted: 'I have said all along that there should not be a knee-jerk reaction or the introduction of sweeping new blanket powers that would ultimately be ineffective'.[253] Unfortunately, the TEO powers appear to have been just that. They reflect a misplaced emphasis on returning foreign terrorist fighters rather than on those who have not sought to participate in the conflicts abroad. Hence, they have not been able to prevent recent domestic terrorist attacks inspired—but not instigated or directed—by Islamic State.

4.5 Families of Foreign Terrorist Fighters

An ancillary consideration relates to the families of suspected foreign terrorist fighters. The question of what governments can and will do in these circumstances is complex. The answer needs to balance the perceived threat of returning foreign terrorist fighters and their families, reintegration and deradicalisation, the application of human rights law (at least in the UK) and domestic criminal sanctions, as well as dealing with political and practical hurdles.

There are many instances in which the families of Australian and UK foreign terrorist fighters have travelled to Islamic State-controlled areas. The best known of these in Australia is the family of Khaled Sharrouf.[254] One year after Sharrouf travelled to Syria, his wife Tara Nettleton and their five children joined him. One of their daughters subsequently became the apparent second wife of—and had a child with—foreign terrorist fighter, Mohamed Elomar.[255] Nettleton, Sharrouf, two of their sons, and Elomar have reportedly all died, leaving the remaining children and grandchild stranded in Syria.[256] They are amongst an estimated 70 Australian children[257] and at least 50 children from the UK[258] who were taken by their foreign terrorist fighter parents to Syria and Iraq or were born in the conflict zones. The return of these families poses a significant challenge. Many of these children may have been exposed to radical militarism and violence. In some cases, they have even been recruited as child soldiers.[259] It is an issue which both the Australian and UK Prime Ministers have suggested should be dealt with on a case by case basis, recognising that the children of foreign terrorist fighters did not instigate their own participation in the conflict.[260] Australian Minister for Immigration, Peter Dutton, has, however, repeatedly expressed concerns over the potential threat that the return of these children would pose to national security. He stated that the Australian Government needs to be cautious in deciding whether to allow them to do so.[261] It is not clear under what power Dutton proposes to exclude these children. His comments imply that simply not assisting their return is an option, as Australia has no diplomatic presence in Syria.[262] However, if they travel to a neighbouring country where Australia has a diplomatic presence or to a country that wishes to deport them, there would seem at present to be no legal way for Australia to deny their return unless, of course, the child is over 14, a dual citizen, and there is sufficient evidence to revoke their citizenship.[263] Furthermore, it is unclear whether Australia could ever develop an exclusion regime that falls short of citizenship revocation to cover such circumstances. This is because the right to abode is arguably protected by the Constitution.[264] The reality is that this issue is unlikely to be resolved by the High Court of Australia until the Australian Government passes and applies a law abrogating this potential right.[265]

If there is a constitutional right of abode for Australian citizens, the effect of any exclusion measures would necessarily be limited to non-citizens. As a result, preventing the return of children may not be possible unless the facts first support deprivation of their citizenship under the Citizenship Act. In the UK, the situation is somewhat different due to the Home Secretary's power to exclude citizens. However, TEOs are still likely to prove ineffective in excluding children. This is because the criteria will often be inapplicable, namely, that the child has been directly involved in terrorism, that this involvement was intentional and not under duress, and that it is now necessary to impose the TEO on this child to protect the domestic public from the risk of terrorism.

4.6 Conclusions

Since 2014, Australia and the UK have introduced and amended a range of legislative measures to prevent foreign terrorist fighters from leaving to participate in the Syrian and Iraqi conflicts, and to prevent their subsequent return. Similarly to its approach with criminal and hybrid measures, the Australian Government has legislated heavily and reactively, often imitating or drawing inspiration from the UK. The UK has also extended the application of its anti-terrorism legislation, strengthening existing powers of police officers, border officials, and the Home Secretary. In preventing the exit of aspiring foreign terrorist fighters, both countries have focused their efforts on security at borders and ports as well as the suspension, refusal, cancellation, and seizure of passports and travel documents. However, in contrast to the criminal and hybrid measures, the UK has not relied purely on legislation. The cancellation and refusal of passports as well as the exclusion of foreign nationals fall within the scope of the royal prerogative, meaning that the Home Secretary has broader and more flexible powers.

The main method of preventing the return of foreign terrorist fighters has been citizenship revocation. Both countries have granted the relevant Ministers extensive discretion to determine whether to revoke citizenship, with neither embedding substantial accountability, transparency, or review provisions. In the UK, citizenship revocation extends so far as to make an individual with sole UK citizenship stateless; although, this specific power has not yet been employed. Indeed, notwithstanding the purported necessity for enacting these laws, they have not been extensively used. In Australia, only one person has had their citizenship revoked. In the UK, the numbers are higher, but the introduction of the TEO regime suggests that citizenship revocation has not proven to be the one-stop solution for dealing with foreign terrorist fighters. Even the TEO regime has only been used at most 'several' times since its enactment.

The limited use of these measures raises considerable doubt over both their initial necessity as well as their effectiveness in practice. We acknowledge that a lack of use does not equate with uselessness. However, for the purposes of this chapter and this book, assessment of a measure's effectiveness is reliant on that measure's ability to achieve its desired result. This chapter has shown how many of the new measures have been unable to achieve their desired result. As exemplified by Australia's citizenship revocation regime, practical challenges have, in many instances, impeded implementation.

Furthermore, where measures have little to no deterrent effect—as is the case with TEOs—low levels of use are even more likely to correlate with the measure's low effectual capacity. It is notable that passport cancellations and foreign travel restraints have also not proved infallible: Siddhartha Dhar reached Syria despite the demanded surrender of his passport, Khaled Sharrouf left Australia on his brother's passport, and Brooks and Keeler left the UK without even possessing passports.

Notes

1 Anti-Terrorism, Crime and Security Act 2001 (UK) ss 21–3.
2 For example, the establishment of control orders in both Australia and the UK: Criminal Code Act 1995 (Cth) div 104; Prevention of Terrorism Act 2005 (UK).
3 As under Australian Passports Act 2005 (Cth) ss 12–14, 16.

4 Ibid., ss 12(1), 13(1), 14.
5 Ibid., s 22A.
6 Ibid., ss 6(1), 24A.
7 Counter-Terrorism Legislation Amendment (Foreign Fighters) Act 2014 (Cth) s 130; Foreign Passports (Law Enforcement and Security) Act 2005 (Cth) ss 15A(1), 16A(1), (5).
8 Australian Passports Act 2005 (Cth) s 24A(2).
9 Explanatory Memorandum, Counter-Terrorism Legislation Amendment (Foreign Fighters) Bill 2014 (Cth) [43].
10 Ibid.
11 Australian Passports Act 2005 (Cth) s 22A(2)(a); Foreign Passports (Law Enforcement and Security) Act 2005 (Cth) s 15A(1)(a) (emphasis added).
12 Australian Passports Act 2005 (Cth) s 22A(3).
13 Foreign Passports (Law Enforcement and Security) Act 2005 (Cth) s 14(1)(a).
14 Explanatory Memorandum, Counter-Terrorism Legislation Amendment (Foreign Fighters) Bill 2014 (Cth) [48].
15 Bret Walker, 'Annual Report' (28 March 2014) Recommendation V/4.
16 Senate Standing Committee for the Scrutiny of Bills, Parliament of Australia, *Fourteenth Report of 2014* (2014) 749.
17 Ibid., 749.
18 Ibid.
19 Ibid., 750.
20 Ibid.
21 Ibid.
22 PJCHR, *Examination of Legislation in Accordance with the Human Rights (Parliamentary Scrutiny) Act 2011*, No 14 of 44th Parliament (2014) [1.244].
23 *International Covenant on Civil and Political Rights,* opened for signature 16 December 1966, 999 UNTS 171 (entered into force 23 March 1976) art. 12.3.
24 Explanatory Memorandum, Counter-Terrorism Legislation Amendment (Foreign Fighters) Bill 2014 (Cth) [49].
25 PJCHR, *Examination of Legislation in Accordance with the Human Rights (Parliamentary Scrutiny) Act 2011*, No 14 of 44th Parliament (2014) [1.241]–[1.245].
26 Australian Passports Act 2005 (Cth) s 50(3).
27 Administrative Decisions (Judicial Review) Act 1977 (Cth) sch 1 s 3(dc) excludes decisions about the suspension and surrender of passports made under the Australian Passports Act 2005 (Cth) from judicial review.
28 Australian Passports Act 2005 (Cth) s 48A.
29 Commonwealth, *Parliamentary Debates*, House of Representatives, 1 September 2016, 338 (Julie Bishop, Minister for Foreign Affairs).
30 Chris Uhlmann, 'ASIO Warns Tourists and Expats of Terrorist Threat in South-East Asia', *ABC News*, 3 March 2017 <www.abc.net.au/news/2017-03-03/asio-warns-of-threats-in-south-east-asia/8323604>.
31 Ibid. See also Bret Walker, 'Annual Report' (28 March 2014) 44.
32 See Chapter 2 at 25.
33 See Chapter 2 at 32.
34 Dominic Casciani, 'Who Is Siddhartha Dhar?', *BBC News*, 4 January 2016 <www.bbc.com/news/uk-35225636>.
35 Neelima Choahan, 'Sevdet Besim, 19, Gets 10 Years' Jail for Anzac Day Plot to Behead Police Officer', *The Age*, 5 September 2016 <www.theage.com.au/

victoria/sevdet-besim-19-gets-10-years-jail-for-anzac-day-plot-to-behead-police-officer-20160905-gr8u95.html>.

36 Tammy Mills, 'Passport Scrutiny Drove Sevdet Besim to Plan Local Attack on "Enemies of Islam"', *The Age*, 12 July 2016 <www.theage.com.au/victoria/passport-scrutiny-drove-sevdet-besim-to-plan-local-attack-on-enemies-of-islam-20160712-gq3zuq.html>.

37 Ibid.

38 Ibid.

39 Rachael Connors, 'Anzac Day Terror Plot: Blackburn Boy Sentenced to Life', *BBC News*, 2 October 2015 <www.bbc.com/news/uk-34423984>.

40 Nick Miller, 'The Boy Who Wanted to Spread Blood and Terror in the Anzac Day Parade', *Sydney Morning Herald*, 3 October 2015 <www.smh.com.au/world/the-who-wanted-to-blow-up-the-anzac-day-parade-20151001-gjz2av.html>.

41 Counter-Terrorism and Security Act 2015 (UK) sch 1 s 1. This includes the border with Northern Ireland, and travel between Britain and Northern Ireland and rail link of Channel Tunnel.

42 Home Office, 'Examining Officers and Review Officers under Schedule 7 to the Terrorism Act 2000: Code of Practice' (March 2015) [23].

43 Counter-Terrorism and Security Act 2015 (UK) sch 1 s 2(8).

44 Counter-Terrorism and Security Act 2015 (UK) sch 1 s 5.

45 Ibid., sch 1 ss 1(12), 8.

46 Ibid., sch 1 s 5(1).

47 Ibid., sch 1 s 4. If this permission is not granted, the passport must be returned to its owner. The only exception is if another (independent) legal action commences in the meantime, for example criminal proceedings: at sch 1 s 7.

48 The officer must be of a higher rank than the senior police officer who initially authorised the passport retention and, at a minimum, of the rank of chief superintendent: ibid., sch 1 s 6(2).

49 Ibid., sch 1 s 9. Legal aid can be granted under ss 1(2)–(3).

50 Ibid., sch 1 s 10.

51 Home Office, 'Examining Officers and Review Officers Under Schedule 7 to the Terrorism Act 2000: Code of Practice' (March 2015) [76], Annex D.

52 Ibid.

53 Counter-Terrorism and Security Act 2015 (UK) sch 1 s 8(4).

54 Home Office, 'Examining Officers and Review Officers under Schedule 7 to the Terrorism Act 2000: Code of Practice' (March 2015) [62].

55 Jessie Blackbourn and Clive Walker, 'Interdiction and Indoctrination: The Counter-Terrorism and Security Act 2015' (2016) 79 *Modern Law Review* 840, 847–9.

56 Counter-Terrorism and Security Act 2015 (UK) s 44.

57 Explanatory Notes, Counter-Terrorism and Security Bill 2015 (UK) 5 [23], 9 [48].

58 Counter-Terrorism and Security Act 2015 (UK) sch 1 s 13.

59 Jessie Blackbourn and Clive Walker, 'Interdiction and Indoctrination: The Counter-Terrorism and Security Act 2015' (2016) 79 *Modern Law Review* 840, 848.

60 Ibid. See *Tower Hamlets London Borough Council v M* [2015] EWHC 869 (Fam); *In re X (Children)* [2015] EWHC 2265 (Fam); *Tower Hamlets London Borough Council v B* [2015] EWHC 2491 (Fam).

61 Home Office, *HM Government Transparency Report 2017: Disruptive and Investigatory Powers*, Cm 9420 (2017) 24.

62 Tim Shipman, Richard Kerbaj, and Dipesh Gadher, 'Ministers Strip 150 Jihadists of UK Passports', *The Sunday Times*, 30 July 2017 <www.thetimes.co.uk/article/ministers-strip-150-jihadists-of-uk-passports-53fn899w2>.

63 Shiv Malik et al., 'British Teenage Jihadi Believed to Have Been Killed in Syria', *Guardian*, 25 September 2014 <www.theguardian.com/world/2014/sep/24/british-teenage-jihadi-believed-killed-syria-ibrahim-kamara>.

64 Counter-Terrorism Act 2008 (UK) s 58, sch 5. As of 2014, there has also been a general power to seize a cancelled passport, and failure to surrender a suspended or cancelled passport is a criminal offence: Anti-Social Behaviour, Crime and Policing Act 2014 (UK) s 147, sch 8.

65 Ibid., s 6.

66 Ibid., s 45. This can include foreign convictions: *Commissioner of Police of the Metropolis v Ahsan* [2016] 1 WLR 654, 665–6 [33].

67 Anti-Social Behaviour, Crime and Policing Act 2014 (UK) pt 4. Under s 44, a person will need to comply with notification requirements if they are over 16 and have been made subject to a 'triggering' sentence (defined in s 45 to include most sentences of 12 months or more). These notification requirements include giving the police your address, photograph, and fingerprints, and notifying the police of any changes to your personal details or of any plans to travel overseas for more than three days.

68 Ibid., sch 5 s 2.

69 Central Criminal Court, 8 January 2016, discussed in David Anderson, 'The Terrorism Acts in 2015' (December 2016) 122.

70 Police did not assume that the pair was travelling for terrorism purposes, but to visit family.

71 David Anderson, 'The Terrorism Acts in 2015' (December 2016) 122.

72 *Attorney-General v De Keyser's Royal Hotel Ltd* [1920] 1 AC 508, 526.

73 See Robert S. Lancy, 'The Evolution of Australian Passport Law' (1982) 13 *Melbourne University Law Review* 428, 434–6.

74 United Kingdom, *Parliamentary Debates*, House of Commons, 25 April 2013, vol. 561, cols 68WS–70WS (Theresa May, Home Secretary).

75 Ibid.

76 Ibid.

77 Ibid.

78 See Home Affairs Committee, *Roots of Violent Radicalisation*, House of Commons Paper No 19, Session 2010–12 (2012) 12 [23]; Chris Angus, 'Radicalisation and Violent Extremism: Causes and Responses' (E-Brief 1/2016, NSW Parliamentary Research Service, February 2016) 4–6 <www.parliament.nsw.gov.au/researchpapers/Documents/radicalisation-and-violent-extremism-causes-and-/Radicalisation%20eBrief.pdf>.

79 [2017] 2 WLR 1437.

80 Ibid., [94].

81 Home Affairs Committee, *Counter-Terrorism*, House of Commons Paper No 17, Session 2013–14 (2014) 36 [95].

82 Home Office, *HM Government Transparency Report 2017: Disruptive and Investigatory Powers*, Cm 9420 (2017) 23.

83 Revised Explanatory Memorandum, Counter-Terrorism Legislation Amendment (Foreign Fighters) Bill 2014 (Cth) [288].

84 Statement of Compatibility, Counter-Terrorism Legislation Amendment (Foreign Fighters) Bill 2014 (Cth) 58.

85 Customs Act 1901 (Cth) s 219ZJA.

86 Ibid., s 219ZJB(1)(b).
87 Ibid., s 219ZJCA.
88 See Gilbert + Tobin Centre of Public Law, Submission No 3 to the PJCIS, *Advisory Report on the Counter-Terrorism Legislation Amendment (Foreign Fighters) Bill*, 1 October 2014, 23.
89 PJCHR, Parliament of Australia, *Examination of Legislation in Accordance with the Human Rights (Parliamentary Scrutiny) Act 2011* (2014) [1.316]–[1.317].
90 Senate Standing Committee for the Scrutiny of Bills, Parliament of Australia, *Fourteenth Report of 2014* (2014) 816–17.
91 As in Crimes Act 1914 (Cth) s 15GE.
92 Criminal Code Act 1995 (Cth) s 80.2C.
93 Ibid., s 119.7.
94 Ibid., s 119.2.
95 Ibid., s 102.8.
96 Revised Explanatory Memorandum, Counter-Terrorism Legislation Amendment (Foreign Fighters) Bill 2014 (Cth) [299] (emphasis added).
97 Senate Standing Committee for the Scrutiny of Bills, Parliament of Australia, *Fourteenth Report of 2014* (2014) 816–17.
98 See PJCIS, *Advisory Report on the Counter-Terrorism Legislation Amendment (Foreign Fighters) Bill* (2014) Recommendation 31.
99 Statement of Compatibility, Counter-Terrorism Legislation Amendment (Foreign Fighters) Bill 2014 (Cth) 58.
100 Senate Standing Committee for the Scrutiny of Bills, Parliament of Australia, *Fourteenth Report of 2014* (2014) 816–17.
101 Australian Passports Act 2005 (Cth) s 32(2).
102 Home Office, *HM Government Transparency Report 2017: Disruptive and Investigatory Powers*, Cm 9420 (2017) 16.
103 David Anderson, 'The Terrorism Acts in 2015' (December 2016) 40–1.
104 Ibid., 41 [7.10].
105 Ibid., 40 [7.9], 41 [7.14].
106 Ibid.
107 Home Affairs Committee, *Radicalisation: The Counter-Narrative and Identifying the Tipping Point*, House of Commons Paper No 8, Session 2016–17 (2016) 24 [79].
108 David Anderson, 'The Terrorism Acts in 2011' (June 2012) 112 [9.50]; *Beghal v DPP* [2016] AC 88, 105 [23].
109 *Beghal v DPP* [2016] AC 88, 105 [22]. See also David Anderson, 'The Terrorism Acts in 2011' (June 2012) 112 [9.48].
110 David Anderson, 'The Terrorism Acts in 2013' (July 2014) 45 [7.11], 46 [7.14].
111 David Anderson, 'The Terrorism Acts in 2011' (June 2012) 115 [9.61].
112 HM Government, *CONTEST, the United Kingdom's Strategy for Countering Terrorism: Annual Report for 2015*, Cm 9310 (2016) [2.35].
113 Migration Act 1958 (Cth) ss 501(1)–(2).
114 Ibid., s 501(6).
115 Department of Immigration and Border Protection, *Why Don't I Meet the Character Requirement?* Australian Government <www.border.gov.au/Lega/Lega/Form/Immi-FAQs/are-there-any-other-reasons-i-might-not-meet-the-character-requirement>.
116 No visa is required for New Zealand citizens and citizens of another 40 or so countries are eligible for either the eVisitor or an Electronic Travel Authority instead of a formal visa.

117 Migration Act 1958 (Cth) ss 134A–134F.
118 Revised Explanatory Memorandum, Counter-Terrorism Legislation Amendment (Foreign Fighters) Bill 2014 (Cth) [314].
119 Migration Act 1958 (Cth) s 134C(5).
120 Ibid., s 134D. The Minister can, however, vary the visa, at his or her discretion: at s 134D(2).
121 *Extremist Brigitte Would Never Be Issued an Australian Visa Says Government* (Australian Visa Bureau, 3 December 2009) <www.visabureau.com/australia/news/03-12-2009/extremist-brigitte-would-never-be-issued-an-australian-visa-says-government.aspx>.
122 Home Office, *HM Government Transparency Report 2017: Disruptive and Investigatory Powers*, Cm 9420 (2017) 24.
123 Edward Christian, John Frederick Archbold, and Joseph Chitty (eds), *Commentaries on the Laws of England: By the Late Sir W. Blackstone, to Which Is Added an Analysis by Barron Field* (Philadelphia: J Grigg, 1827) 194.
124 Home Office, *HM Government Transparency Report 2017: Disruptive and Investigatory Powers*, Cm 9420 (2017) 24.
125 'Britain Bans Saudi Cleric Who Supports Jihad in Syria', *Reuters UK*, 26 June 2014 <http://uk.reuters.com/article/uk-britain-islam-saudi-cleric/britain-bans-saudi-cleric-who-supports-jihad-in-syria-idUKKBN0F024R20140625>.
126 *Directive 2004/38/EC on the Right of Citizens of the Union and Their Family Members to Move and Reside Freely Within the Territory of the Member States* [2004] OJ L 158/77.
127 Ibid., arts 27(1)–(2). The UK's withdrawal from the EU in 2019 may affect the position of European Economic Area nationals and their families.
128 *P I v Oberbürgermeisterin der Stadt Remscheid* (Court of Justice of the European Union, C-348/09, 22 May 2012) [28].
129 *Straszewski v Secretary of State for the Home Department* [2016] 1 WLR 1173, 1182 [20].
130 *P I v Oberbürgermeisterin der Stadt Remscheid* (Court of Justice of the European Union, C-348/09, 22 May 2012) [17].
131 European Operational Policy Team, 'Assessing Applications in Accordance with Public Policy, Public Security or Public Health' (Policy Notice 01/2013, Home Office, 5 February 2013) <www.gov.uk/government/uploads/system/uploads/attachment_data/file/309048/30748_-_Annex_4_-_Notice_01-2013_Public_Policy_and_Public_Security__revised__-_redacted.pdf>.
132 Sharri Markson, 'IS Supporters Free to Return to Australia Despite Tough Law Changes', *The Daily Telegraph*, 2 March 2017 <www.dailytelegraph.com.au/news/nsw/is-supporters-free-to-return-to-australia-despite-tough-law-changes/news-story/8480f28ce58a7304e47e94e390fcad44>.
133 'Theresa May: Online Extremism "Must Be Tackled"', *BBC News*, 26 May 2017 <www.bbc.co.uk/news/election-2017-40052471>.
134 *Potter v Minahan* (1908) 7 CLR 277.
135 Indigenous Australian Callum Clayton-Dixon was permitted to enter Australia even though the Aboriginal 'passport' he presented at Brisbane airport was not recognised as valid: Cameron Atfield, 'Aboriginal Passport the First Step to Independence, Says Activist Callum Clayton-Dixon', *Brisbane Times*, 25 April 2015 <www.brisbanetimes.com.au/national/queensland/aboriginal-passport-the-first-step-to-independence-says-activist-callum-claytondixon-20150423-1ms1xi.html>.
136 Australian Citizenship Act 2007 (Cth) s 34.

137 Australian Citizenship Amendment (Allegiance to Australia) Act 2015 (Cth).
138 Commonwealth, *Parliamentary Debates*, House of Representatives, 30 November 2015, 14116 (Peter Dutton, Minister for Immigration and Border Protection).
139 Australian Citizenship Act 2007 (Cth) ss 33AA(2)(b), (c), (e), (h).
140 Ibid., s 33AA(3).
141 Ibid., s 33AA(4).
142 Ibid., s 33AA(9).
143 Ibid., ss 33AA(14)–(17).
144 Ibid., s 33AA(7).
145 Ibid., ss 35(1)(c), 35(9)–(12).
146 Ibid., s 35AA(2). A 'declared terrorist organisation' under this section has a different meaning to the lists under s 102.1(1) of the Criminal Code or s 15 of the UN Charter Act.
147 Ibid., s 35(4).
148 Ibid., s 35A(1). If the individual's conviction is later overturned in a non-appealable judicial decision, the Minister must undo the citizenship cessation by revoking the initial determination: at s 35A(8).
149 Ibid., s 35A(1)(e).
150 Ibid., s 52.
151 Department of Immigration and Border Protection, Submission No 37.4 to the PJCIS, *Inquiry into the Australian Citizenship Amendment (Allegiance to Australia) Bill 2015*, August 2015, 2–3.
152 See 'Note' under Australian Citizenship Act 2007 (Cth) ss 33AA(10), 35(5), 35A(1).
153 Australian Citizenship Act 2007 (Cth) s 35B.
154 Ibid., ss 33AA(15), (20), 35(10), (15), 35A(10).
155 For discussion on the legal fiction that is a self-executing law, both generally and in this context, see *Australian Postal Corporation v Forgie* (2003) 130 FCR 279, 285 [26], 291 [56]; Evidence to PJCIS, Canberra, 4 August 2015, 14 (George Williams); Evidence to PJCIS, Canberra, 5 August 2015, 44 (Helen Irving).
156 Paul Farrell, 'Government Officials of Secretive Citizenship Loss Board Named', *Guardian*, 22 July 2016 <www.theguardian.com/australia-news/2016/jul/22/government-members-of-secretive-citizenship-loss-board-named>.
157 Revised Explanatory Memorandum, Australian Citizenship Amendment (Allegiance to Australia) Bill (2015) 18 [67], 25 [119], 33 [162], 39 [202], 44 [236].
158 Department of Immigration and Border Protection, *Citizenship Loss Board IDC* (Australian Government) <www.border.gov.au/AccessandAccountability/Documents/FOI/20160520_FA160401379_Documents_Released.pdf>.
159 Jane Norman and Caitlyn Gribbin, 'Islamic State Fighter Khaled Sharrouf Becomes First to Lose Citizenship Under Anti-terror Laws', *ABC News*, 11 February 2017 <www.abc.net.au/news/2017-02-11/islamic-state-fighter-khaled-sharrouf-stripped-of-citizenship/8262268>.
160 Ellen Whinnett, 'Government Eyes 18 Australian Jihadis to Citizenship Revocation', *Herald Sun*, 16 September 2015 <www.heraldsun.com.au/news/victoria/government-eyes-18-australian-jihadis-to-citizenship-revocation/news-story/6f4e633b53add1f1dfee8175149a5920>.
161 Sharri Markson, 'IS Supporters Free to Return to Australia Despite Tough Law Changes', *The Daily Telegraph*, 2 March 2017 <www.dailytelegraph.com.au/

news/nsw/is-supporters-free-to-return-to-australia-despite-tough-law-changes/
news-story/8480f28ce58a7304e47e94e390fcad44>.

162 Joseph Chamie, 'Unwanted Immigrants: America's Deportation Dilemma', *Yale Global: Yale Center for the Study of Globalisation*, 27 July 2010 <http://yaleglobal. yale.edu/content/unwanted-immigrants-americas-deportation-dilemma>.

163 Susan Jones, 'ICE Director: "Bunch" of Countries Refuse U.S. Efforts to Deport Criminal Aliens', *CNS News*, 3 December 2015 <www.cnsnews. com/news/article/susan-jones/ice-director-bunch-countries-refuse-us-efforts-deport-criminal-aliens>.

164 Ron Nixon, 'Trump Administration Punishes Countries that Refuse to Take Back Deported Citizens', *New York Times*, 13 September 2017 <www.nytimes. com/2017/09/13/us/politics/visa-sanctions-criminal-convicts.html>.

165 Jon Boone, 'Pakistan Sends Deported Migrants Back to Greece', *Guardian*, 4 December 2015 <www.theguardian.com/world/2015/dec/03/pakistan-sends-deported-migrants-back-to-greece-eu>.

166 Sune Engel Rasmussen, 'EU Signs Deal to Deport Unlimited Numbers of Afghan Asylum Seekers', *Guardian*, 4 October 2016 <www.theguardian.com/ global-development/2016/oct/03/eu-european-union-signs-deal-deport-unlimited-numbers-afghan-asylum-seekers-afghanistan>.

167 David Anderson, 'Citizenship Removal Resulting in Statelessness' (April 2016) 15 [3.14].

168 Sharri Markson, 'IS Supporters Free to Return to Australia Despite Tough Law Changes', *The Daily Telegraph*, 2 March 2017 <www.dailytelegraph.com.au/ news/nsw/is-supporters-free-to-return-to-australia-despite-tough-law-changes/ news-story/8480f28ce58a7304e47e94e390fcad44>.

169 Australian Citizenship (Declared Terrorist Organisation—Islamic State) Declaration 2016 (Cth); Australian Citizenship (IMMI 17/073: Declared Terrorist Organisation—Jabhat Al-Nusra) Declaration 2017 (Cth).

170 British Nationality Act 1948 (UK) ss 20(3), (5). This is the avenue of citizenship revocation most relevant to the denationalisation of foreign fighters. There are also other bases on which citizenship can be deprived—where the person acquired the citizenship by means of fraud, false representation, or concealment of a material fact: at ss 40(3), (6).

171 See Nationality, Immigration and Asylum Act 2002 (UK) s 4, amending the British Nationality Act 1981 (UK) s 40; Immigration, Asylum and Nationality Act 2006 (UK) s 56.

172 'Full Text: The Prime Minister's Statement on Anti-Terror Measures', *Guardian*, 5 August 2005 <www.theguardian.com/politics/2005/aug/05/uksecurity. terrorism1>.

173 British Nationality Act 1981 (UK) ss 40(2), (4).

174 Home Office, *HM Government Transparency Report 2017: Disruptive and Investigatory Powers*, Cm 9420 (2017) 24.

175 HM Government, *National Security Strategy and Strategic Defence and Security Review 2015: A Secure and Prosperous United Kingdom*, Cm 9161 (2015) 37–40.

176 Ibid., 40–2.

177 HM Government, *National Security Strategy and Strategic Defence and Security Review 2015: First Annual Report 2016* (December 2016) 19–26.

178 Ibid., 27–30.

179 Home Affairs Committee, *Counter-terrorism and Community Relations in the Aftermath of the London Bombings: Oral and Written Evidence* (13 September 2005) Q28 (Charles Clarke).
180 Ibid., Annex B.
181 'Cleric Stripped of Citizenship', *BBC News*, 5 April 2003 <http://news.bbc.co.uk/1/hi/uk/2919291.stm>.
182 *Abu Hamza v Secretary of State for the Home Department* (Unreported, Special Immigration Appeals Commission, 5 November 2010).
183 *Al-Jedda v Secretary of State for Home Department* [2014] AC 253.
184 Ibid., 260 [4].
185 Ibid., 261 [8].
186 Ibid. The Home Office was refused permission to introduce evidence that his Iraqi passport had been used to travel, and that the Iraqi Government regarded him as a citizen. Accordingly, the Home Office issued another deprivation order on 1 November 2013. SIAC decided as a preliminary issue that this second deprivation order did not render Mr Al-Jedda stateless contrary to s 40(4) of the British Nationality Act 1981 (UK).
187 David Anderson, 'Citizenship Removal Resulting in Statelessness' (April 2016) 8 [2.17].
188 Explanatory Notes, Immigration Bill 2014 (UK) 8 [32].
189 United Kingdom, *Parliamentary Debates*, House of Commons, 7 May 2014, vol. 580, col. 198 (James Brokenshire).
190 House of Commons Library, *Deprivation of British Citizenship and Withdrawal of Passport Facilities* (Briefing Paper No 06820, 9 June 2017) 21 n 30 citing *Al-Jedda v Secretary of State for the Home Department* (Unreported, Special Immigration Appeals Commission, 18 July 2014); appeal dismissed by the Court of Appeal on 24 March 2017 (Unreported).
191 British Nationality Act 1981 (UK) s 40(4A)(b).
192 Home Office, 'Immigration Bill, Fact Sheet: Deprivation of Citizenship (Clause 60)' (January 2014).
193 British Nationality Act 1981 (UK) s 40(4A)(c).
194 *Al-Jedda v Secretary of State for Home Department* [2014] AC 253, 266 [23].
195 Ibid.
196 British Nationality Act 1981 (UK) s 40(5).
197 David Anderson, 'Citizenship Removal Resulting in Statelessness' (April 2016) 15–16 [3.18]. Anderson notes that this is in stark contrast to other executive powers, such as TPIMs and Temporary Exclusion Orders.
198 British Nationality Act 1981 (UK) ss 40A(6)–(8), as repealed by Asylum and Immigration (Treatment of Claimants, etc) Act 2004 (UK) sch 1 pt 4(c).
199 Such direction will be made by either the First Tier Tribunal (Immigration and Asylum Chamber) or SIAC, depending on where the appeal is heard.
200 House of Commons Library, *Deprivation of British Citizenship and Withdrawal of Passport Facilities* (Briefing Paper No 06820, 9 June 2017) 16.
201 'Theresa May's Speech on Terrorism and Extremism—Full Text and Audio', *The Spectator*, 30 September 2014 <https://blogs.spectator.co.uk/2014/09/theresa-mays-speech-on-terrorism-and-extremism-full-text-and-audio/>.
202 *Convention on the Reduction of Statelessness*, opened for signature 30 August 1961, 989 UNTS 175 (entered into force 13 December 1975) art. 8(3)(a)(ii). The UK ratified the Convention in March 1966 with reservation as to art. 8.

203 Home Office, *HM Government Transparency Report 2017: Disruptive and Investigatory Powers*, Cm 9420 (2017) 26.

204 United Kingdom, *Parliamentary Debates*, House of Commons, 30 January 2014, vol. 574, col. 1038 (Theresa May, Home Secretary).

205 David Anderson, 'Citizenship Removal Resulting in Statelessness' (April 2016) 4.

206 Ibid., 14 [3.10], citing Letter of James Brokenshire to the Joint Committee on Human Rights, 20 February 2014, Question 10.

207 House of Commons Library, *Deprivation of British Citizenship and Withdrawal of Passport Facilities* (Briefing Paper No 06820, 9 June 2017) 10.

208 Victoria Parson, *Theresa May Deprived 33 Individuals of British Citizenship in 2015* (Bureau of Investigative Journalism, 21 June 2016) <www.thebureau investigates.com/stories/2016-06-21/citizenship-stripping-new-figures-reveal-theresa-may-has-deprived-33-individuals-of-british-citizenship>.

209 Home Office, 'FOI Release: Individuals Deprived of British Citizenship Since 2013' (18 December 2014) <www.gov.uk/government/publications/individuals-deprived-of-british-citizenship-since-2013/individuals-deprived-of-british-citizenship-since-2013>.

210 Tim Shipman, Richard Kerbaj, and Dipesh Gadher, 'Ministers Strip 150 Jihadists of UK Passports', *The Sunday Times*, 30 July 2017 <www.thetimes.co.uk/article/ministers-strip-150-jihadists-of-uk-passports-53fn899w2>.

211 Victoria Parson, *Theresa May Deprived 33 Individuals of British Citizenship in 2015* (Bureau of Investigative Journalism, 21 June 2016) <www.thebureau investigates.com/stories/2016-06-21/citizenship-stripping-new-figures-reveal-theresa-may-has-deprived-33-individuals-of-british-citizenship>.

212 *K2 v United Kingdom* (European Court of Human Rights, Chamber, Application No 42387/13, 9 March 2017).

213 Ibid., [6].

214 Ibid., [57].

215 Kent Roach and Craig Forcese, 'Why Stripping Citizenship Is a Weak Tool to Fight Terrorism', *The Globe and Mail*, 3 March 2016 <www.theglobeand mail.com/opinion/why-stripping-citizenship-is-a-weak-tool-to-fight-terrorism/article29003409/>.

216 SC Resolution 1373, UN SCOR, 4385th mtg, UN Doc S/RES/1373 (28 September 2001); SC Resolution 2178, UN SCOR, 7272nd mtg, UN Doc S/RES/2178 (24 September 2014); SC Resolution 2170, UN SCOR, 7242nd mtg, UN Doc S/RES/2170 (15 August 2014); SC Resolution 2322, UN SCOR, 7831st mtg, UN Doc S/RES/2322 (12 December 2016).

217 Kent Roach and Craig Forcese, 'Why Stripping Citizenship Is a Weak Tool to Fight Terrorism', *The Globe and Mail*, 3 March 2016 <www.theglobeand mail.com/opinion/why-stripping-citizenship-is-a-weak-tool-to-fight-terrorism/article29003409/>.

218 See Home Office, *HM Government Transparency Report 2017: Disruptive and Investigatory Powers*, Cm 9420 (2017) 24.

219 See this chapter at 69.

220 Cat Barker, 'Citizenship Revocation on National Security Grounds: Context and Selected Issues' (Research Paper Series 201516, Parliamentary Library, Parliament of Australia, 2015) 13.

221 Barak Mendelsohn, 'Foreign Fighters—Recent Trends' (2011) 55 *Orbis* 189, 191.

222 Jewel Topsfield 'Australia Warns of "Regional IS Caliphate" Ahead of Meeting on Terror Threat', *Sydney Morning Herald*, 28 July 2017 <www.smh.com.au/world/australia-warns-of-regional-is-caliphate-ahead-of-meeting-on-terror-threat-20170728-gxkucd.html>.
223 SC Resolution 1373, UN SCOR, 4385th mtg, UN Doc S/RES/1373 (28 September 2001).
224 *Thomas v Mowbray* (2007) 233 CLR 307.
225 SC Resolution 1546, UN SCOR, 4987th mtg, UN Doc S/RES/1546 (8 June 2004).
226 *R (Al-Jedda) v Secretary of State for Defence* [2008] AC 332.
227 Conditions A–E in Counter-Terrorism and Security Act 2015 (UK) ss 2(3)–(7).
228 Ibid., ss 2(1), 4(9).
229 Ibid., s 5.
230 Ibid., s 9.
231 Ibid., s 10(5).
232 United Kingdom, *Parliamentary Debates*, House of Commons, 1 September 2014, vol. 585, col. 31 (David Cameron, Prime Minister).
233 Ibid., col. 26 (David Cameron, Prime Minister).
234 Ibid.
235 Commonwealth, *Parliamentary Debates*, House of Representatives, 14 November 2014, 12710–15 (David Cameron, Prime Minister).
236 Theresa May, 'Home Secretary Theresa May on Counter-Terrorism' (Speech delivered at RUSI, London, 24 November 2014) <www.gov.uk/government/speeches/home-secretary-theresa-may-on-counter-terrorism>.
237 Immigration Act 1971 (UK) s 2(1)(b).
238 Guy Goodwin-Gill, '"Temporary Exclusion Orders" and Their Implications for the United Kingdom's International Legal Obligations, Part I', *EJIL: Talk!* 8 December 2014 <www.ejiltalk.org/temporary-exclusion-orders-and-their-implications-for-the-united-kingdoms-international-legal-obligations-part-i/>.
239 Evidence to Joint Committee on Human Rights, UK Parliament, London, 26 November 2014, Q8 (David Anderson).
240 Ibid.
241 Home Office, 'Counter-Terrorism and Security Act 2015—Temporary Exclusion Orders—Royal Assent' (Impact Assessment No HO0144, 11 February 2015) <www.gov.uk/government/uploads/system/uploads/attachment_data/file/540545/Temporary_Exclusion_IA_Royal_Assent_MASTER_COPY.pdf>.
242 Peter Walker, 'Rudd Admits Anti-Terror Exclusion Powers Used Only Once Since 2015', *Guardian*, 29 May 2017 <www.theguardian.com/uk-news/2017/may/29/uk-used-anti-terror-exclusion-powers-once-since-2015-amber-rudd-admits>. See also Clive Walker, 'Foreign Terrorist Fighters and UK Counter-Terrorism Laws', in David Anderson, 'The Terrorism Acts in 2015' (December 2016) Annex 2, 121; Home Office, *HM Government Transparency Report 2017: Disruptive and Investigatory Powers*, Cm 9420 (2017) 25.
243 Tim Shipman, Richard Kerbaj, and Dipesh Gadher, 'Ministers Strip 150 Jihadists of UK Passports', *The Sunday Times*, 30 July 2017 <www.thetimes.co.uk/article/ministers-strip-150-jihadists-of-uk-passports-53fn899w2>.
244 HM Government, *CONTEST, the United Kingdom's Strategy for Countering Terrorism: Annual Report for 2015*, Cm 9310 (2016) [2.35].
245 A Freedom of Information request to the Home Office requesting annual figures of returned foreign terrorist fighters was denied on the grounds that the public

interest in disclosing the material did not outweigh the risk to national security: FOI Request No 42967 (14 March 2017).

246 David Anderson, 'The Terrorism Acts in 2015' (December 2016) 10.

247 Vikram Dodd and Esther Addley, 'Leytonstone Knife Attack: Man Convicted of Attempted Murder', *Guardian*, 9 June 2016 <www.theguardian.com/uk-news/2016/jun/08/leytonstone-knife-attack-man-convicted-of-attempted>.

248 Ian Cobain, 'Jo Cox Killed in "Brutal, Cowardly" and Politically Motivated Murder, Trial Hears', *Guardian*, 15 November 2016 <www.theguardian.com/uk-news/2016/nov/14/jo-cox-killed-in-politically-motivated-murder-trial-thomas-mair-hears>.

249 David Anderson, 'The Terrorism Acts in 2015' (December 2016) 11.

250 Temporary Exclusion Orders (Notices) Regulations 2015 (UK) SI 2015/438, reg 3(1)(a).

251 Counter-Terrorism and Security Act 2015 (UK) s 4(1); ibid., reg 3(1).

252 *Temporary Exclusion Orders (Notices) Regulations 2015* (UK) SI 2015/438, reg 3(2).

253 United Kingdom, *Parliamentary Debates*, House of Commons, 1 September 2014, vol. 585, col. 25 (David Cameron, Prime Minister).

254 See Chapter 2 at 33.

255 See Chapter 2 at 26.

256 'Khaled Sharrouf, Australian Terrorist, Believed to Have Been Killed in Air Strike in Syria', *ABC News*, 17 August 2017 <www.abc.net.au/news/2017-08-16/khaled-sharrouf-believed-to-have-been-killed/8812600>.

257 James Renwick, 'Sections 119.2 and 119.3 of the Criminal Code: Declared Areas' (September 2017) 22.

258 Noman Benotman and Nikita Malik, 'The Children of Islamic State' (Quilliam International, 7 March 2016) 8 <www.quilliaminternational.com/quilliam-releases-report-on-children-in-the-caliphate/>.

259 See Francesca Capone, 'Child Soldiers: The Expanding Practice of Minors Recruited to Become Foreign Fighters', in Andrea de Guttry, Francesca Capone, and Christophe Paulussen (eds), *Foreign Fighters Under International Law and Beyond* (The Hague: TMC Asser Press, 2016).

260 ABC, 'Should Homesick Islamic State and Other Foreign Fighters Be Allowed to Return?', *7.30*, 19 May 2015 (Leigh Sales) <www.abc.net.au/7.30/content/2015/s4238750.htm>; Stuart McLean, 'Vile Jihadist Khaled Sharrouf in New Atrocity Showing Son Posing with Dead Man', *The Daily Telegraph*, 7 May 2017 <www.dailytelegraph.com.au/news/nsw/vile-jihadist-khaled-sharrouf-in-new-atrocity-showing-son-posing-with-dead-man/news-story/066ae05ddb6b3debc8935152afc03739>.

261 Liz Burke, 'Why Terrorist's Daughter Zaynab Sharrouf Needs to Get Out of Syria', *news.com.au*, 21 March 2016 <www.news.com.au/national/why-terrorists-daughter-zaynab-sharrouf-needs-to-get-out-of-syria/news-story/15d505f66 3ab1d17bff088b61af4549f>.

262 Helen Irving, 'Even Khaled Sharrouf's Family Has the Right to Come Home', *The Conversation*, 30 June 2015 <https://theconversation.com/even-khaled-sharroufs-family-has-the-right-to-come-home-44019>.

263 Passport cancellation could also be a mode of exclusion, unless there is a constitutional right of abode of Australian citizens: see n 265.

264 Helen Irving, 'Still Call Australia Home: The Constitution and the Citizen's Right of Abode' (2008) 30 *Sydney Law Review* 133. Some scholarship has

questioned the ease with which this conclusion can be reached: Sangeetha Pillai, 'Non-immigrants, Non-Aliens and People of the Commonwealth: Australian Constitutional Citizenship Revisited' (2013) 39 *Monash University Law Review* 568; Sangeetha Pillai, 'The Rights and Responsibilities of Australian Citizenship: A Legislative Analysis' (2014) 37 *Melbourne University Law Review* 736, 758–65.

265   The idea of a citizen's right of abode was raised in the recent High Court hearings about the dual citizenship of a number of Australian parliamentarians. Counsel for Nick Xenophon claimed that he was not a dual citizen at the time of nomination, and hence was not ineligible under s 44(i) of the Constitution. This was because he was merely a British Overseas Citizen and, accordingly, had no right of entry into and/or abode in the UK. In its unanimous judgment, the High Court engaged positively with this submission: one of the reasons why Xenophon was ultimately not disqualified under s 44(i) was that his status '[did] not confer the rights or privileges of a citizen as that term is generally understood: a [British Overseas Citizen] does not have the right to enter or reside in the United Kingdom': *Re Canavan; Re Ludlam; Re Waters; Re Roberts [No 2]; Re Joyce; Re Nash; Re Xenophon* [2017] HCA 45 [131]. While not going towards the question of whether the rights of entry and abode are constitutionally protected in Australia, the judgment does emphasise the High Court's view of these rights as core to citizenship.

5 Lessons

5.1 Efforts to 'Defeat' Terrorism Are Misguided

Statements made by the Australian and UK Governments in responding to the foreign terrorist fighters phenomenon identify the ultimate goal as being to eliminate terrorism in its entirety. After touring the site of the terrorist attack at London Bridge with his UK counterpart, the Australian Prime Minister, Malcolm Turnbull, expressed the intention of both countries as being to 'stand up, defy [the terrorists] and defeat them as we are doing in the field'.[1] Similar statements have been made by the UK Prime Minister, Theresa May. In her speech to the House of Commons immediately after that same attack, she stated:

> It is so important that we show that it is our values that will prevail, that the terrorists will not win and that we will go about our lives showing that unity of purpose and the values that we share as one nation as we go forward, ensuring that the terrorists will be defeated. . . . We must defeat, of course, the terrible ideology that leads people to conduct these horrific attacks.[2]

Whilst such statements are clearly rhetorical in character, underpinning them is nevertheless a fundamental misunderstanding on the part of the authorities regarding the place of terrorism throughout history. The foreign terrorist fighters phenomenon is certainly novel in terms of the sheer number of Westerners involved in the Syrian and Iraqi conflicts as well as the use by Islamic State of social media to rapidly spread its message and attract new recruits from all over the world. However, terrorism existed prior to the declaration of a caliphate by Islamic State and will continue to exist well after the disintegration of that organisation.

It is not only terrorism in general which has a long history. There have also been innumerable precursors to the modern iteration of the foreign terrorist fighters phenomenon, especially in recent decades. For example, in 1976, a Committee of Privy Counsellors was appointed to inquire into the recruitment of 160 British mercenaries to serve with the National Liberation Front of Angola against the People's Movement for the Liberation of Angola.[3] Since then, significant numbers of people from the UK have participated in foreign conflicts, including the 'anti-Soviet jihad' in Afghanistan in the 1980s, the religio-nationalist conflict in the Balkans in the 1990s, and, finally, in Afghanistan and Iraq in response to the campaigns conducted by the US and its allies after the September 11 terrorist attacks.[4] There is also evidence of Australian involvement in each of these conflicts, with the exception of that in the Balkans.[5]

Given the above, it is misguided for the Australian and UK authorities to take action on the basis that it will ever be possible to eliminate terrorism in its entirety.[6] This is a lesson that the UK should already have learned from its experience of countering terrorism in Northern Ireland. The conflict there officially ended in 1998, when a peace agreement between the main protagonists was reached.[7] Violence has, however, not ceased altogether. Terrorist organisations have killed more than 100 people in the 20 years since the peace agreement was reached.[8] Instead, we must recognise the threat which terrorism presents as having a permanent place in society. Acceptance of this means that Australian and UK authorities will no longer be chasing—and the public in those counties no longer demanding—the achievement of an impossible goal. In turn, this will facilitate a more restrained and proportionate response to the challenges posed by the foreign terrorist fighters phenomenon and the threat of terrorism generally.

5.2 The Default Response Has Been to Enact New Legislation

In addressing the foreign terrorist fighters phenomenon, the response of the Australian and UK Parliaments has typically been to enact new, or add to existing, legislation. Since the enactment of its first raft of national anti-terrorism legislation in 2002, the pattern in Australia has continued to be one of reactive, rather than restrained, lawmaking. In response to the July 2005 London bombings, the Australian Federal Parliament passed unprecedented laws allowing for the issuing of control orders and preventative detention orders.[9] These laws were subsequently amended in the aftermath of the Paris terrorist attacks in November 2015.[10] Roger Wilkins, a former Secretary of the Attorney-General's Department, commented: 'The take-out message [from Paris] for me is that the response, the use of control orders, needs to be much stronger. In a modern, liberal democracy that's about the only thing you can do'.[11] He continued, in relation to the proposal to lower the age at which a person can be subject to a control order from 16 to 12, that control orders were 'the best and most sensible way of dealing with the problem' of increasingly younger people being involved in terrorism.[12]

As this book clearly demonstrates, this is not the only instance in which Australia has modified its legislative framework in response to the foreign terrorist fighters phenomenon. The declaration of a caliphate by Islamic State was immediately followed by several rafts of legislation, which involved, amongst other things, the creation of new criminal offences and substantial tightening of border security.[13] In the last year alone, modifications have been made to bail and parole regimes in many Australian States and Territories in response to the revelation that the perpetrator of the June 2017 siege in a Melbourne apartment building had previously been acquitted of a terrorism offence and was on parole for using force to enter a property.[14] At the time of writing, other proposals which are being considered include the following: extending the period of pre-charge detention from eight to 14 days;[15] introducing a new offence of possessing instructional material;[16] and, allowing the Australian Security Intelligence Organisation (ASIO) to detain an individual without a judicial warrant.[17]

It is undoubtedly appropriate in the aftermath of an incident which threatens community safety or national security, such as a terrorist attack, to reflect critically upon the current legislative framework and consider whether any improvements should be made. The key point, however, is that the introduction of new legislation or amending existing legislation must not simply be a knee-jerk reaction. Such steps should be targeted at substantive gaps in the legislative framework which the incident has served to reveal. The failure on the part of the Australian authorities to utilise legislative measures adopted in response to the foreign terrorist fighters phenomenon, such as the offence of advocating terrorism,[18] demonstrates that those measures were not necessary to fill a gap in the pre-existing legislative framework. Of course, such assessments are always available as a matter of hindsight. It must be acknowledged that restraint in enacting new measures is easy to urge, but much harder to put into practice, when the security of the public, the country, and the international community may be put at risk by making the wrong decision not to act.

The reality, however, is that even prior to the emergence of the foreign terrorist fighters phenomenon, both Australia and the UK had extensive anti-terrorism legislative regimes in place. This means that their legislative responses are targeting increasingly smaller gaps, and—as the next section will discuss—the returns are also diminishing. This has been recognised by the Independent Reviewer of Terrorism Legislation (IRTL), Max Hill. In responding to a proposal that jail terms of up to 15 years should be imposed on people who repeatedly view terrorist content online, he stated: 'In general, I would suggest that our legislators, parliament, have provided for just about every descriptive action in relation to terrorism, so we should pause before rushing to add yet more offences to the already long list'.[19]

Recent terrorist attacks in the UK have revealed just how small these gaps in the legislative framework have become. For example, the Westminster Bridge terrorist attack in March 2017 prompted the UK Government to consider introducing a new measure requiring rental companies to conduct additional security checks on any person who wants to hire a vehicle.[20] Even without the benefit of hindsight, the limited utility of such a measure is clear. Whilst it might be of some assistance to the authorities in circumstances where a terrorist sought to hire a vehicle to use in an attack, it will be of no use whatsoever where they pursue other means of procuring vehicles, such as through theft or hijacking, as was the case in relation to the December 2016 attack on a Christmas market in Berlin. This measure would also be useless against a terrorist who had sufficient funds to purchase a vehicle for use in an attack. There is also the additional issue of the practical difficulties—both for the UK authorities and the car hire company—in conducting checks of every person who wants to hire a vehicle. As became clear in the aftermath of the terrorist attack at the Manchester Arena, the perpetrator, Salman Abedi, was potentially one of more than 20,000 people who had come to the attention of the UK authorities.[21] However, he was not then, and nor had he ever been, the subject of an active investigation. Unless a measure like that described above was extended to all persons who had ever come to the attention of the authorities, it is difficult to see how it could ever be effective in preventing terrorism. However, if it was so extended, the time and human resources needed by the authorities to carry out the checks would render the measures unworkable in practice.

Under the Westminster system, upon which both the Australian and UK constitutional frameworks are based, the potential for the enactment of unnecessary and disproportionate legislation is supposedly minimised by the traditions of responsible and representative government. However, in the atmosphere of hysteria which emerges in the aftermath of a terrorist attack, the public often places irresistible pressure on legislators for protection from both actual as well as perceived threats. In such circumstances, the public may act as a catalyst for, rather than a check upon, the creation and use of extraordinary legislative powers. The quickest and most overt way for a government to be seen to be addressing public fears is through the introduction of legislation. Whilst the very nature of democracy means that this is an understandable response, it is also, in many instances, short-sighted. For example, the irrationality of the Australian Federal Parliament's response to the Paris attacks is thrown into sharp relief by the advice from European security analysts that those attacks were due to intelligence failures rather than any gaps in the legislative framework.[22] They occurred in spite of the extensive surveillance powers of French law enforcement and intelligence agencies.

The pattern of reactive lawmaking in the aftermath of terrorist attacks may be contrasted with what Laura Donohue terms a 'culture of restraint'.[23] As described by Donohue, such a culture 'resists extraordinary procedures and encourages the immediate institution of an inquiry following a terrorist attack' or another threat to the security of the State or its citizens.[24] Whilst the establishment of such a culture may appear idealistic in the absence of external pressure, for example, from an international human rights instrument, to do so, the critical point is that this is a worthwhile goal to strive towards. The responsibility of parliaments should be to 'negotiate the relationship between representative democracy and the pressure of terrorism', 'to fix what is actually broken [in the legislative framework] and to introduce new laws in a deliberate fashion'.[25] Far from undermining security, recalibrating official responses such that the enactment of legislation is the exception, rather than the rule, is likely to result in a legislative framework that is more appropriately adapted to the goals it is trying to pursue.

5.3 More Legislation Does Not Necessarily Correlate to Greater Levels of Security

The primary purpose of this book has been to evaluate the effectiveness of legislative responses to the foreign terrorist fighters phenomenon. From the perspective of the authorities, there are four distinct purposes to these—and indeed any other—types of responses. The particular weight placed on each purpose has differed from jurisdiction to jurisdiction and shifted over the course of the three and a half years since the declaration of a caliphate by Islamic State. The first purpose is the prevention of Australian and UK citizens and residents from joining the Syrian and Iraqi conflicts. The second is to maintain tight controls on the immigration system such that individuals who have obtained combat experience overseas or been radicalised there are not able to return undetected. Third, and in the alternative, the responses are aimed at prosecuting those who travel overseas to join the conflicts or provide other forms of support (whether at home or overseas) to the individuals and terrorist organisations involved. The final purpose is to minimise the risk presented by sympathisers of Islamic State, Al-Qaida, and their affiliates on domestic soil.

The legislative measures adopted to achieve these purposes have not been uncontroversial. One of the primary reasons is the impact of those measures on civil liberties. The control order and TPIMs regimes, for example, undermine the principle at the heart of the criminal justice system that a person should not be detained except as a consequence of a finding of criminal guilt.[26] Furthermore, the inclusion of minors as young as 14 under the

Australian regime potentially violates international norms relating to the rights of the child.[27] Legislative measures permitting the revocation of citizenship and exclusion of citizens from their home country also arguably fall foul of international human rights norms, as well as domestic protections.[28] The Universal Declaration of Human Rights states that no one may be arbitrarily deprived of their nationality.[29] This does not mean that citizenship can never be revoked but rather that the circumstances of revocation must be specified in legislation and that there are sufficient safeguards so as to ensure that a person is not rendered stateless.[30] Human rights arguments have, however, been notoriously unsuccessful in influencing policymaking in the counter-terrorism space. The UK Government, like that in Australia, has recently considered extending the period of pre-charge detention from 14 to 28 days.[31] The UK Prime Minister, Theresa May, commented in relation to objections presented by human rights advocates: '[I]f human rights laws stop us from doing it, we will change those laws so that we can do it'.[32]

Whilst the impact upon civil liberties is an obvious basis for critique, it is not the only reason for the controversy surrounding the legislative responses to the foreign terrorist fighters phenomenon. To use the language of effectiveness relied upon by legislators themselves, this book demonstrates that many of the measures adopted or modifications made have been of little utility. They have had limited success in achieving the four purposes outlined above, and therefore have not led to any marked increase in national security or community safety. This is not simply because the measures add little of substance to the pre-existing legislative framework, but also because of the inherent limitations of the law itself. Reliance upon the criminal law, for example, is predicated upon foreign terrorist fighters returning to domestic soil or attempted foreign terrorist fighters acting recklessly so as to bring themselves to the attention of the authorities.[33]

In so far as prosecutions of those who travel overseas to join the Syrian and Iraqi conflicts are concerned, the new Australian offence of being in a declared terrorist area, which was introduced in 2014 and ostensibly tailored to the specifics of the foreign terrorist fighters phenomenon, was not utilised for more than three years after it came into effect. Even then, it has been relied upon once only. A similar result is likely to occur if the Australian Government's proposal to create an offence of possession of instructional material is endorsed by the Federal Parliament.[34] This is because the proposed offence substantially overlaps with that in s 101.4 of the Criminal Code of possessing a thing connected with preparation for, the engagement of a person in, or assistance in a terrorist act. The strong trend in both Australia and the UK has been to rely upon offences which pre-dated the declaration of a caliphate by Islamic State. In the UK, the focus has been upon the offences of doing an act in preparation for terrorism, encouraging terrorism and disseminating a terrorist publication. The Australian authorities have reached even further into the past by relying upon the foreign incursions offences which were introduced in the late 1970s. What can be taken from this, especially in the Australian context, is that in spite of the repeated claims by parliamentarians that gaps in the anti-terrorism criminal regime increased the risk posed by foreign terrorist fighters, filling these gaps has proven to be relatively ineffectual. To the extent that legislation is ever going to make us safer, this has been achieved by the pre-caliphate laws.

Such remarks about lack of use are equally applicable beyond the criminal context. First, the UK has only used its TEO powers a handful of times since they were established in 2015.[35] This is despite approximately 400 foreign terrorist fighters having returned from the Syrian and Iraqi conflicts. A TEO was also not even considered in the case of the UK's only known returned foreign terrorist fighter to engage in a terrorist attack, Salman Abedi.[36] Second, none of the many amendments made by the Australian Federal Parliament to the control order regime since the start of the Syrian and Iraqi conflicts have been utilised.[37] The regime as it existed in early 2014 would have been sufficient to authorise the four control orders issued in the foreign terrorist fighters era. Finally, the citizenship revocation power has been utilised by the Australian authorities on one occasion only, in respect of Khaled Sharrouf.[38] The use of the citizenship revocation power has been more frequent in the UK. However, one of the greatest controversies of this regime is that it does nothing to mitigate the foreign terrorist fighter threat. Its effect is merely to displace that threat, most likely to Syria and Iraq. The ongoing conflicts in those countries mean that foreign terrorist fighters are extremely unlikely to be detained, charged, and prosecuted. Instead, the strong likelihood is that they will resume their participation in those conflicts and will be free, should they so wish, to plot or inspire attacks against the West.

Apart from being ineffective, the citizenship revocation example demonstrates that there is the potential for the legislative measures adopted by the Australian and UK Parliaments to be counter-productive, in the sense that their primary effect is to shift the locale of a terrorist attack. A tightening of border controls in both Australia and the UK, including by way of expanding pre-existing powers to suspend and cancel travel documents, has undoubtedly disrupted some individuals' travel plans and thus prevented them from engaging in, or supporting, terrorism overseas.[39] For others, such as Sevdet Besim, it merely displaced that activity to domestic soil.[40] Unable to leave Australia to participate in the Syrian and Iraqi conflicts, Besim turned his attention to domestic terrorism and planned to behead a police officer at the 2015 Anzac Day parade in Melbourne. In this instance, not only did the enactment of new laws not serve to increase the security of Australia, it had the opposite effect. Besim is just one of a number of young people who have been prosecuted for terrorism offences in recent years. Even more young people are under investigation by, or on the radar of, the AFP and ASIO. There is clearly a bigger issue at play here, and one that the criminal law is not necessarily able to deal with.

Similarly, the ever-increasing number of anti-terrorism laws, and the corresponding burdens which they impose upon law enforcement and intelligence agencies to investigate relatively trivial matters, has the potential to undermine the ability of those agencies to perform their central functions. This is indeed one of the dangers inherent in the proposal discussed above to check the backgrounds of every person wishing to hire a vehicle. The challenge of finding 'a needle in a haystack', especially when it is not even clear that a needle is in fact there, is something that has been commented upon in the context of stop and search powers in the UK,[41] as well as the thousands of calls made to counter-terrorism hotlines.[42]

5.4 Need for a Shift in Thinking

There can be no denying that the foreign terrorist fighters phenomenon represents a significant threat to global stability, national security, and community safety. This is not something that can be ignored. Nor can we—despite accepting that the threat posed by terrorism has a permanent place in society—fail to respond. The fundamental question therefore is how to respond in a manner which both respects the values upon which Australian and British society are based and is effective in mitigating against the threat. A discussion paper published by the Home Office in 2004 noted:

> There is no greater challenge for a democracy than the response it makes to terrorism. The economic, social and political dislocation which sophisticated terrorist action can bring threatens the very democracy which protects our liberty. But that liberty may be exploited by those supporting, aiding or engaging in terrorism to avoid pre-emptive intervention by the forces of law and order. The challenge, therefore, is how to retain long-held and hard-won freedoms and protections from the arbitrary use of power or wrongful conviction whilst ensuring that democracy and the rule of law itself are not used as a cover by those who seek its overthrow.[43]

Following the September 11 terrorist attacks, Australia enacted its first national anti-terrorism laws. Whilst controversial at the time,[44] it is now widely—albeit not universally—accepted that the distinctive nature of terrorism means that a specific body of legislation is appropriate. Since then, however, there has been increasing awareness, especially in academic circles, that legislation is only one part of the equation. The 'hard power' mentality embodied in the legislative responses to the foreign terrorist fighters phenomenon in both Australia and the UK is not an adequate response in and of itself. To be effective, it must be complemented by other 'softer' initiatives. This is so not only because of the inherent limitations, and even counterproductive effects, of legislation, but also the specific advantages which such initiatives bring to the table.

'Soft power' is a concept developed by Joseph Nye to describe the use of persuasion rather than coercion to obtain compliance.[45] Both the Australian and UK Governments have come a long way over the last two decades in recognising the role which soft initiatives are capable of playing in combating terrorism. Each implemented programmes in the mid-2000s aimed at countering violent extremism.[46] These initially emphasised social cohesion and community integration, and in Australia in particular, they had a strong focus on encouraging Muslim communities to participate more in mainstream sporting, social, and cultural activities. Over time, the focus of these programmes shifted towards building resilient communities, and identifying and supporting individuals at risk of 'radicalisation'.[47] In response to the foreign terrorist fighters phenomenon, the focus has shifted again, this time towards deradicalisation. In Australia, early intervention programmes have been designed to prevent those most at risk of radicalisation from engaging in violent extremist conduct, specifically 'to support individuals who perhaps were contemplating travelling to participate in foreign conflicts, had returned or perhaps had been frustrated in their attempts to travel overseas'.[48] In the UK, public bodies have been placed under a statutory duty to prevent vulnerable persons from being drawn into terrorism, including by referring them to the UK's flagship deradicalisation programme, Channel.[49]

A range of criticisms have been levelled at the manner in which soft initiatives have been implemented in Australia and the UK. The most fundamental of these is that they continue to be regarded by governments as a 'backup' option. As the ongoing pattern of reactive lawmaking in Australia and the UK so clearly demonstrates, the enactment or modification of legislation remains the default response in both jurisdictions. Even in the rare instances where soft initiatives are placed front and centre, the statutory grounding of these initiatives, as well as their emphasis upon the involvement of governmental authorities, introduces an element of coercion into the programmes which has the potential to undermine their persuasive effect. As the former IRTL, David Anderson, said: 'There is a strong feeling in Muslim communities that I visit that Prevent is if not a spying programme then at least a programme that is targeted on them'.[50]

Despite these criticisms, credit must be given where it is due. The recognition on the part of the Australian and UK Governments that minimising the risk of terrorism requires a combination of approaches is undeniably a step in the right direction. The proliferation of terrorist attacks in both jurisdictions in 2017 sends the clear message that in spite of the ever-increasing number of laws on the statute books, they are not having the desired preventive effect. The above criticisms point to pathways forward for the refinement and expansion of soft initiatives. These include commissioning further research on the root causes of terrorism and, on the back of this, developing tools for early identification of young people at risk of radicalisation, as well as outsourcing soft initiatives to community groups to remove the risk of them being seen as government-operated 'spying programme[s]'.[51] The critical lesson for governments is the need to think laterally about how to combat the threat of terrorism, rather than continually reworking existing—and demonstrably unsuccessful—strategies.

The focus of this book has been upon the effectiveness of legislative responses to the foreign terrorist fighters phenomenon specifically. By focusing upon a single facet of the terrorist threat, the intention of the authors has been to engage deeply with the practical application of these responses so as to assess the extent to which they have contributed to an increase in security at both the domestic and global levels. The micro nature of this analysis does not, however, mean that its relevance is tied to the continuation of the Syrian and Iraqi conflicts. Far from it. The significance of this book lies in its highlighting of some of the erroneous assumptions upon which counter-terrorism strategy in Australia and the UK is based. These include, in particular, the assertion that terrorism can be eliminated in its entirety, as well as the unspoken belief that legislation is the best means of achieving this. The prevalence of such thinking has the potential to impede the development of effective policies in the counter-terrorism space not only in the present, but also into the future. As Australian Labor parliamentarian, Anne Aly, has noted:

> Daesh is but one iteration of a global violent jihadist movement that is likely to continue even after the last operative is gone from Syria and Iraq. This is not the fight of my generation but the fight of generations to come, and we need to keep paying attention to it.[52]

The foreign terrorist fighters phenomenon may be the most recent terrorist crisis to throw up challenges for Australia and the UK, but history clearly demonstrates that it will not be the last. Whilst this book is far from the final word on the matter of the foreign terrorist fighters phenomenon, and indeed barely scratches the surface so far as alternatives to legislation are concerned, it is the hope of the authors that it will serve as a useful jumping-off point for discussions about how to foster a more sophisticated manner of both thinking about, and responding to, the threat posed by terrorism.

Notes

1 Malcolm Turnbull, 'Press Conference—London' (Transcript, 11 June 2017) <www.pm.gov.au/media/2017-07-11/press-conference-london>.

2 United Kingdom, *Parliamentary Debates*, House of Commons, 23 March 2017, vol. 623, col. 941 (Theresa May, Prime Minister).

3 HM Government, *Report of the Committee of Privy Counsellors Appointed to Inquire into the Recruitment of Mercenaries*, Cmnd 6569 (1976).

4 Maria Galperin Donnelly, 'Foreign Fighters in History' (Center for Strategic and International Studies, 2017).

5 Andrew Zammit, 'Australian Foreign Fighters: Risks and Responses' (Lowy Institute for International Policy, April 2015) 8.

6 The current INSLM, James Renwick, noted that 'there can be no guarantee that the authorities will detect and prevent all attacks': James Renwick, 'Sections 119.2 and 119.3 of the Criminal Code: Declared Areas' (September 2017) 7.

7 HM Government, *The Belfast Agreement: An Agreement Reached at the Multi-Party Talks on Northern Ireland*, Cm 3883 (1998).

8 David McKittrick et al. (eds), *Lost Lives: The Stories of the Men Women and Children Who Died as a Result of the Northern Ireland Troubles* (Edinburgh: Mainstream Publishing, 2007) 1552; CAIN, *Draft List of Deaths Related to the Conflict from 2002 to the Present* (23 January 2017) <http://cain.ulst.ac.uk/issues/violence/deathsfrom2002draft.htm>.

9 Anti-Terrorism Act (No 2) 2005 (Cth).

10 Counter-Terrorism Legislation Amendment Act (No 1) 2016 (Cth).

11 Rachel Olding and David Wroe, 'Control Orders "Must Be Extended" to Avoid Paris-Style Attack in Australia', *Sydney Morning Herald*, 18 November 2015 <www.smh.com.au/national/control-orders-must-be-extended-to-avoid-paris-style-attack-in-australia-20151117-gl0yz0.html>.

12 Ibid.

13 National Security Legislation Amendment Act (No 1) 2014 (Cth); Counter-Terrorism Legislation Amendment (Foreign Fighters) Act 2014 (Cth); Telecommunications (Interception and Access) Amendment (Data Retention) Act 2015 (Cth).

14 See Terrorism Legislation Amendment (Police Powers and Parole) Act 2017 (NSW).

15 Sabra Lane, Interview with Malcolm Turnbull (Radio Interview on *ABC AM*, 4 October 2017) <www.pm.gov.au/media/2017-10-04/radio-interview-sabra-lane-abc-am>.

16 COAG, 'Special Meeting of the Council of Australian Governments on Counter-Terrorism' (Communiqué, 5 October 2017) <www.coag.gov.au/sites/default/files/communique/special-communique-20171005.pdf> 2.

17 ASIO, Supplementary Submission No 8.6 to PJCIS, *Review of ASIO's Questioning and Detention Powers*, 4 September 2017, 9.

18 See Chapter 2 at 11–2, 30.

19 'UK Terrorism Law Expert Warns Government over Plans for New Legislation', *Guardian*, 25 October 2017 <www.theguardian.com/politics/2017/oct/24/uk-terrorism-government-plans-new-legislation-laws-max-hill>.

20 Gwyn Topham, 'UK Considering Extra Checks for Van Hire to Deter Terrorist Attacks', *Guardian*, 21 August 2017 <www.theguardian.com/uk-news/2017/aug/20/uk-extra-checks-for-van-hire-to-deter-terrorist-attacks-watch-list>.

116   *Lessons*

21 See Chapter 1 at 1–3.
22 Griff Witte and Loveday Morris, 'Failure to Stop Paris Attacks Reveals Fatal Flaws at Heart of European Security', *The Washington Post*, 28 November 2015 <www.washingtonpost.com/world/europe/paris-attacks-reveal-fatal-flaws-at-the-heart-of-european-security/2015/11/28/48b181da-9393-11e5-befa-99ceebcbb272_story.html?utm_term=.5e5fa1c5e360>.
23 Laura Donohue, *The Cost of Counterterrorism: Power, Politics, and Liberty* (Cambridge: Cambridge University Press, 2008) 336.
24 Ibid.
25 Laura Donohue, 'The Perilous Dialogue' (2009) 97 *California Law Review* 357, 391.
26 See Chapter 3 at 42–3.
27 Megan Mitchell, 'The Human Rights of Children Are at Risk If Control Orders Are Placed on 14-Year-Olds', *Sydney Morning Herald*, 16 October 2015 <www.smh.com.au/comment/the-human-rights-of-children-are-at-risk-if-control-orders-are-placed-on-14yearolds-20151015-gkanfv.html>.
28 See Chapter 4 at 78–86.
29 *Universal Declaration of Human Rights*, GA Res 217A (III), UN GAOR, 3rd sess, 183th mtg, UN Doc A/810 (10 December 1948) art. 15(2).
30 Mirna Adjami and Julia Harrington, 'The Scope and Content of Article 15 of the Universal Declaration of Human Rights' (2008) 27 *Refugee Survey Quarterly* 93, 101.
31 Rowena Mason and Vikram Dodd, 'May: I'll Rip Up Human Rights Laws that Impede New Terror Legislation', *Guardian*, 7 June 2017 <www.theguardian.com/politics/2017/jun/06/theresa-may-rip-up-human-rights-laws-impede-new-terror-legislation>.
32 Ibid.
33 See Chapter 2 at 14–15.
34 COAG, 'Special Meeting of the Council of Australian Governments on Counter-Terrorism' (Communiqué, 5 October 2017) 2 <www.coag.gov.au/sites/default/files/communique/special-communique-20171005.pdf>.
35 See Chapter 4 at 89.
36 See Chapter 4 at 89.
37 See Chapter 3 at 45–51.
38 See Chapter 4 at 80.
39 See Chapter 4 at 65–76.
40 See Chapter 4 at 69.
41 Joint Committee on the Draft Investigatory Bill, *Draft Investigatory Powers Bill Report*, House of Lords Paper No 93, House of Commons Paper No 651, Session 2015–16 (2016) 91–2.
42 Hayden Smith, 'Calls to Terror Tip-off Hotline Surge 600 Per Cent After Wave of UK Attacks', *The Independent*, 16 August 2017 <www.independent.co.uk/news/uk/crime/calls-police-terror-hotline-tip-offs-up-600-per-cent-uk-attacks-a7897346.html>.
43 HM Government, *Counter-Terrorism Powers: Reconciling Security and Liberty in an Open Society: A Discussion Paper*, Cm 6147 (2004) 1.
44 Senate Legal and Constitutional Legislation Committee, Parliament of Australia, *Inquiry into the Security Legislation Amendment (Terrorism) Bill 2002 [No 2] and Related Bills* (2002) 19–25.

45 See Joseph Nye, 'Soft Power' (1990) 80 *Foreign Policy* 153.

46 Ministerial Council on Immigration and Multicultural Affairs, *A National Action Plan to Build on Social Cohesion, Harmony and Security* (2007); HM Government, *Pursue Prevent Protect Prepare the United Kingdom's Strategy for Countering International Terrorism*, Cm 7547 (2009).

47 Australian Government, *Counter-Terrorism White Paper: Securing Australia, Protecting Our Community* (2010); HM Government, *CONTEST: The United Kingdom's Strategy for Countering Terrorism*, Cm 8123 (2011).

48 Commonwealth of Australia, *Senate Estimates* (11 December 2014) 69.

49 Counter-Terrorism and Security Act 2015 (UK) pt 5.

50 Alan Travis, 'Prevent Strategy to Be Ramped Up Despite "Big Brother" Concerns', *Guardian*, 11 November 2016 <www.theguardian.com/uk-news/2016/nov/11/prevent-strategy-uk-counter-radicalisation-widened-despite-criticism-concerns>.

51 Ibid.

52 Commonwealth, *Parliamentary Debates*, House of Representatives, 21 November 2016, 3832 (Anne Aly).

Index

For Product Safety Concerns and Information please contact our EU
representative GPSR@taylorandfrancis.com
Taylor & Francis Verlag GmbH, Kaufingerstraße 24, 80331 München, Germany

www.ingramcontent.com/pod-product-compliance
Ingram Content Group UK Ltd.
Pitfield, Milton Keynes, MK11 3LW, UK
UKHW021422080625
459435UK00011B/125